SEÁN MacBRIDE

A Biography

Anthony J. Jordan

BLACKWATER PRESS

Printed in Ireland at the press of the publishers 1993

© Blackwater Press 1993
Broomhill Industrial Park,
Broomhill Road,
Tallaght,
Dublin 24.

ISBN 0 86121 453 6

The author and publisher wish to thank the following for permission granted to use material:

Institute of Public Administration for *The Irish Department of Finance 1922-1958* by Ronan Fanning and *The Formulation of Irish Foreign Policy by Patrick Keatinge.*
Gill & Macmillan for *Against the Tide* by Noel Browne, *Sean Lemass and the Making of Modern Ireland* by Paul Bew and Henry Patterson.
C.J. Fallon for *Devoy's Postbag* by E. O'Brien and E. Ryan.
Mercier Press for *A Message to the Irish People* by Sean MacBride and *Man of No Property by* C.S. Andrews.

While every effort has been made to contact copyright holders we have failed to contact some. Blackwater Press will be happy to come to some arrangement with these should they wish to contact us.

Typeset by Wendy A. Commins, The Curragh

Contents

Acknowledgements

I would like to thank the following for assistance rendered: staffs of the National Library of Ireland, Royal Dublin Society Library, Pembroke and Ringsend Public Libraries; Louie O'Brien, Muireann McHugh, Anna White and Tiernan MacBride.

I would also like to acknowledge the continued understanding of my wife, Mary, and my daughters, Judith and Fiona (who compiled the index).

This work is dedicated to three people whose courage and perseverance I have admired.

Ciaran Barry
Enda MacDonagh
Conor Cruise O'Brien

Introduction

Seán MacBride spent the first fourteen years of his life in France. His native language was French. His parents had separated in a bitter public divorce case, while he was a baby. Although his mother won custody of her son, she feared returning to live in Dublin while her husband lived. A major influence on the boy was the poet W.B. Yeats. When her husband was executed after the 1916 Rising, Madame MacBride brought Seán to live in Dublin.

She was an ardent nationalist. Her son shared her views. Though still a teenager, he fought in the War of Independence against the British. When the Anglo-Irish Treaty was signed in 1921 Seán MacBride alongside de Valera, opposed it and the resulting native government. He spent the next sixteen years as an active member of the IRA, eventually becoming its Chief of Staff. He was later demoted and became disillusioned with the IRA.

For the next ten years he pursued a legal career, often defending IRA members. He set up a political party Clann na Poblachta, which became part of a coalition government in 1948, ousting Fianna Fáil from power. MacBride became Minister for External Affairs and played a leading inter-national role in post-war reconstruction at the Council of Europe and the OEEC. He negotiated with Attlee, Churchill, Dean Acheson and Harry Truman. He kept Ireland out of NATO and was instrumental in the Declaration of the Irish Republic in 1949.

In 1951 Clann na Poblachta lost public support amid bitter personal recriminations. MacBride evoked adulation from some, but fear and hatred from others. A profile written on him in 1952 by Jack B. Yeats, was both a character assassination and a political obituary.

Though MacBride was never to hold a government ministry again, his influence on the Coalition Government of 1954-1957 was marked. Referring to an Aide-Memoire sent to the British Government by the Department of External Affairs in 1956, Conor Cruise O'Brien writes: 'This document ... clearly reflects the influence of ... Seán MacBride.... It represents what was to remain the high water-mark of Irish government collusion with the IRA'.[1]

In the 1960s MacBride assumed an international role, becoming closely identified with human rights worldwide. He helped found and steer Amnesty International. He worked for the International Commission of Jurists. In the 1970s he was awarded the Nobel Peace Prize, the Lenin Peace Prize and the American Medal of Justice.

During his latter years he again became actively involved in Irish affairs, though in a non party-political way. The continuing war in Northern Ireland, with its Hunger Strikes and endemic violence, captured his attention. His life though full of contradictions, had almost come full circle. He was indeed a kaleidoscopic man ...

1

Maud Gonne Versus John MacBride

Seán MacBride was born on 26 January 1904 in Coleville, Normandy. His birth brought great joy to both his parents, Maud Gonne and Major John MacBride. The event was also of great interest to a wider public in France, Britain, North America and especially Ireland. Many people regarded his stock so highly that he was spoken of as though he was an Irish prince, destined to have a major impact on the future life of the Irish nation. Congratulations poured in from many quarters, one of them addressed to 'Future President of Ireland'. Less than four months later, on May Day, the baby was taken by his mother to be baptised in Dublin. This was an occasion which was to set a precedent for much of Seán's future life. It was observed by the police who compiled a report on the congregation, among whom were many ardent nationalists. The foremost of these was the old Fenian, John O'Leary, who was the choice of both parents to act as the child's godfather. The boy's father was unable to be present lest he be arrested for treasonable offences, connected with his exploits in South Africa.

A note on the Baptismal Register says: 'The child was born in France but his parents wished him to be baptised in the parish of their Irish residence'. This was 26 Coulson Avenue, Rathgar and the church was that of St Joseph's Terenure. He was christened 'Seagan (John, Joannes) Gonne MacBride'. The register names his grandmother, Honoria MacBride, as godmother. There is no godfather listed as the parish priest objected to John O'Leary, who was a well-known agnostic. The officiating priest was Terence Conor Anderson.

Maud Gonne was an Englishwoman, born in 1866, whose

9

father, Tommy, had been a colonel in the British army. He had
been stationed at the Curragh and in Dublin when Maud was
a little girl and again when she was a teenager. While in
Dublin, Maud had much contact with the local ascendancy
community. Her mother had died earlier and she often acted
as hostess at social occasions hosted by her father. She was a
keen rider and took part in many hunts on estates of the
gentry. When she was twenty years old, she and her younger
sister, Kathleen, spent some time in Royat, a spa town in the
Auvergne district of France. There she met and fell in love
with a French nationalist politician named Lucien Millevoye.
They formed a pact to work together for the freedom of Ireland
from the English, and Alsace and Lorraine from the Prussians.
Maud dedicated the rest of her life to the cause of Irish freedom. Through inherited wealth from her mother's family,
Maud became financially independent. She made Paris her
permanent home and continued a long liaison with Millevoye.
They had two children, a boy George (1891) and a girl Iseult
(1894). Much to her horror, her son died in infancy and she
longed for another boy. She had been extremely close to her
deceased father and believed a son of hers would be his rein-
carnation. Over a period of fifteen years, commuting between
France and Ireland, she proved herself to nationalist Ireland
by her hard and even very dangerous work in a wide variety
of fields. She was rightly regarded as an Irish heroine and was
treated as a colleague by all the leading nationalists from
John O'Leary to Arthur Griffith.

John MacBride, born in Westport, County Mayo in 1865,
was a life-long member of the Irish Republican Brotherhood.
His father was of Ulster-Scots stock, from Glenshesk in the
Glens of Antrim. He had been a ship's captain who often sailed
into Westport. When he married a local woman, Honoria Gill,
he left the sea and set up in business on Westport Quay. John
was the youngest of five sons. He had to leave home to find
work and did so in Dublin and eventually (1897) in South
Africa. There he became an Irish hero because of his organisation and co-leadership of the Irish Brigade, which fought
the English in the Boer War. An Irish Transvaal Committee
supported MacBride and the Boers. Maud Gonne and Arthur
Griffith were at its head. When the Irish Brigade disbanded

in 1900, MacBride came to Paris, where he was met by Maud Gonne and Griffith. At this time she had just parted from her French lover. Maud was enthralled to meet an Irishman who had actually taken up arms against the English. John fell headlong in love with her. She, Griffith and John discussed the latter's future. It was decided that he should undertake a lecture tour of the United States of America. John later telegrammed Maud from New York to say that he was quitting the tour unless she joined him. This she readily did and they visited Boston, Philadelphia, St Louis and Chicago together. In St Louis John proposed to her. She prevaricated and after getting a message from Griffith to come to Ireland, she returned to Paris. MacBride continued on to San Francisco and completed the tour himself. He then returned to New York. He could have remained there and have been well placed within the Irish American community. If he returned to Ireland he could face arrest for his activities in the Boer War. Instead he went back to Paris to woo Maud.

Maud Gonne was a wealthy European sophisticate of staggering beauty and proposals of marriage came to her from many eligible bachelors. Her home in Paris was a centre for famous people to meet and be seen. Consternation and disbelief greeted the news that she had accepted the proposal of a penniless Irish political exile. Family friends and nationalist colleagues advised both of them not to marry. They felt that because Maud and John came from such different worlds, a marriage between them was doomed to failure. Arthur Griffith begged them not to marry. At the wedding ceremony in Paris in 1903, performed by Father Van Hecke, chaplain of the Irish Brigade, the flags of Maud's organisation, Daughters of Erin, and John's Irish Brigade were carried.

Seán was born eleven months after the wedding, but already the marriage was in serious trouble. Irreconcilable differences, and her husband's alleged infidelity and drunkenness, had brought Maud to the conclusion that her future and that of her children did not rest with Major MacBride. Early the following year in 1905 she started divorce proceedings, which ended in a judicial separation. Maud's primary concern was to retain custody of her infant son. She tried to get the French court to deny the father access to his son, saying that she feared MacBride might kidnap him and return to Ireland, where he could retain custody. John MacBride agreed to his wife retaining custody, but was granted the right to visit Seán at his wife's home every Monday afternoon for two hours, under supervision. Very shortly afterwards, he decided to risk returning to live in Dublin, never again to have any contact with his wife or son. Maud took no chances with her estranged husband. She spoke only in French to the boy, so that if his father did return, he would not be able to converse with him. Seán MacBride always spoke with a pronounced French accent.

The reporting on the divorce case in Ireland was predictable. Griffith ignored it totally in his newspaper, *United Irishman*, but the other papers reported on it assiduously. It was too good a story to miss. The *Weekly Independent* carried most copy. On 4 March 1905 its headline ran: 'Mrs MacBride Applies for a Divorce'. A PARIS SENSATION. Part of the report read:

The forthcoming suit will, it is understood, centre mainly on the question of the child's guardianship. Mrs MacBride alleges infidelity and intemperance which the husband absolutely denies.

The Major is well known in the Irish and American circles in Paris. He is willing that his wife should have the custody of the child on condition that the boy spends at least nine months of every year in Ireland, in a Catholic and nationalist atmosphere.

The marriage of Miss Gonne caused positive amazement in Paris, for her many friends believed that she had vowed herself to celibacy. Did not her admirers fondly call her the Joan of Arc of Ireland? Certainly suitors had not been wanting and it is doubtful if the heart of Queen Elizabeth herself sustained sieges more gallant and devoted. Irish Poets, French Marquisses, English Officers, American millionaires, Ordinary Members of Parliament, Brilliant artists and Rising Barristers had all known the resistless charms of Miss Gonne's beauty and the fascination of her bewitching smile.

The Major's immediate reason for returning to Dublin in 1906, was to prosecute a libel case he had instituted against the *Irish Independent* for the way it had reported the divorce case. The Dublin jury found in his favour, but all he was awarded was the derisory sum of £1. Nationalist Ireland was sorely divided by the public conflict between two of its heroes.

Maud Gonne did not attend the libel case, though she was legally represented. In October she made her first public appearance in Dublin since the divorce case, attending the first night of Lady Gregory's play 'The Gaol Gate' at the Abbey Theatre. In her book *Life and the Dream*, Mary Colum, who was in the audience, recorded the theatrical scene:

> Ten, fifteen minutes passed and the curtain did not go up. Somebody or some thing was being waited for. At last we saw Yeats enter hastily ... accompanied by a tall woman dressed in black, one of the tallest women I have ever seen. Instantly a small group in the pit began to hiss loudly and to shout 'Up MacBride' ... The woman stood and faced her hissers, her whole figure showing a lively emotion.... Yeats, standing beside her, looked bewildered as the hissing went on: his face was set in lines of gloom, but she was smiling and unperturbed. Soon a counter hissing set up, the first hissers being drowned by another group and then I realised who she was....[1]

Major MacBride too, was well aware of the difficulties created for himself by the separation and attending publicity. One of his immediate problems was to start earning a living. He approached the *Freemans Journal* and offered it a series of articles on his experiences during the Boer War. His first article appeared on 13 October 1906. That same day he wrote to his good friend and mentor, John Devoy of New York, suggesting that Devoy's paper, the *Gaelic American*, might also publish the articles. His letter illustrates how well he realised that it might not be politic for Devoy to be seen to be supporting MacBride at that juncture. The letter reads:

Dublin

13/10/1906

Dear Devoy,

The 'Freeman' is taking four or five articles from me on the Irish Brigade and I would be glad, if you would think it advisable, if the *Gaelic American* would insert them. I sent you the first which appeared today.

As you are aware it was my intention to write an account of the Irish Brigade for the *Gaelic American*: but recent events made me think it would be better if I could get the *Freeman* to publish them. Of course the more notice that is taken of them now, the more chance I will have of getting in other articles afterwards. You will understand though, that if you consider that it would be better for the *Gaelic American* not to touch them, or me, I will feel in no way hurt or offended. I received word from the *Freeman* that I must avoid politics and moderate my language. They cut several good things out of my first ...

Sincerely yours,
John MacBride.[2]

The police had not bothered the Major since his return to Ireland and he decided to remain at home. Neither his journalistic career, nor any other career, flourished. He tried hard to get gainful employment. The next four years were a very difficult period for him, as he struggled to survive. All the while he had to observe his wife continue her practice of coming to Ireland regularly in pursuit of her nationalistic work. She continued to maintain a Paris home and was most reluctant to bring her son to Ireland, lest his father reclaim the boy.

It was not until 1910 that John MacBride was successful in getting a permanent job. That year the Dublin Corporation employed him as a water bailiff. His duties consisted of collecting dues from ships using the river Liffey. He continued to be closely associated with those who were planning an insurrection. The Local City of Dublin Unionist Association tried to have him dismissed from his post because of his inflammatory public speeches. The Corporation maintained that his political views were his own business.[3] MacBride was closely associated with the Irish Republican Brotherhood which was infiltrating the Irish Volunteers and was planning an armed rising as soon as an opportune moment arrived. The IRB did not believe that the Irish Volunteers would of their own volition, take military action against the English.

2

Boyhood in France

Seán MacBride spent his most formative years in an almost exclusively female environment. His home contained many pets, plants and exotic birds. Maud was an artist and it showed in her household. She sold a lot of her watercolours at the Salon des Artistes Independents in Paris. She doted on her son, taking him with her to functions from a very early age, especially if these involved fundraising for the nationalist cause. When she was away, he often stayed with Madame Cama, a famous Indian nationalist. His half-sister Iseult attended a convent boarding school at Laval.

The poet William Butler Yeats had been pursuing Maud Gonne for more than ten years when she married MacBride. He had written some beautiful love poetry about her and his despair after the marriage produced more fine love lyrics. But Yeats was reconciled to Maud within six months of the wedding and soon began to visit and stay at her homes in Paris and Normandy. He observed her son grow up, writing to his friend Lady Gregory: 'I believe I was meant to be the father of an unruly family. I did not think that I liked little boys, but I liked Shawn'.[1]

When Seán was six months old, his mother had taken him and Iseult to Mulraney, County Mayo for a long summer holiday. It was only twenty miles from the MacBride family home in Westport. MacBride's mother welcomed them and idolised the baby. She was so grateful to Maud for bringing her grandson home. Maud wanted to keep on good terms with the MacBrides because her half-sister, Eileen Wilson, was married to Joseph MacBride, John's older brother. Eileen Wilson was the illegitimate daughter of Maud's father, Tommy Gonne. Major MacBride did not appear in Mayo while Maud and her children were there. He lived permanently in Dublin.

When Seán was four, he was sent to school at the Jesuit college, St Louis de Gonzague, on rue Franklin in Paris. His mother, meanwhile, continued her campaigns in Ireland, attempting to make the authorities provide school dinners for children. At about this time, both her children began to complain about being left behind in Paris. Seán was not a very healthy boy and, after a severe bout of measles, he had to be nursed by Maud for several months in 1911. She herself developed pneumonia and was sent to a nursing home in Lourdes.

Like Maud's earlier conversion to Irish nationalism, her conversion to Catholicism, prior to her marriage, was taken very seriously, and her faith became a lifelong commitment. She brought her son up in that faith and he too was quite religious from an early age. He made his First Holy Communion on 19 March 1911, where his name on the group souvenir was Jean Gonne. The next month, Maud and her son were received in a private audience at the Vatican by Pope Pius X. The following morning, Seán assisted at the Pope's mass and he and Maud received Holy Communion from the Holy Father. Two years later, on 21 June 1913, Seán was confirmed by Cardinal Amette, the archbishop of Paris. This was no ordinary mother and child.

Margaret Cousins, an Irish woman active in Indian affairs wrote a 1912 description of Seán at the Coleville house in Normandy saying: 'A young lad, thin, pale and dreamy, was introduced as Shawn.... He disposed of us quickly, we being only human beings, and busied himself over the important matter of the safe transit of a pet bantam cock home in the cart'.[2]

In the spring of 1914 Maud Gonne MacBride took Seán to Dublin to meet Padraig Pearse, the headmaster of St Enda's school where she intended to enrol him in the autumn if the family moved to Dublin. Seán remembered his mother talking to Pearse of the expected world war.

When the Great War broke out, Maud, Seán and Iseult and some friends got stranded at Argeles, in the Pyrennees. They volunteered their services to a local hospital where war casualties were being cared for. The first-hand view of the effects of the war had a tremendous influence on Maud, making her turn against violence and armed conflict. Seán worked as a messenger boy at the hospital. After a few months in Argeles, they returned to Paris, though travel was very difficult and dangerous.

When the Germans threatened Paris, Maud moved to her Normandy house, where W.B. Yeats was a frequent visitor. It was there, after Easter 1916, that Maud first heard of the Rising in Dublin. In May she was told that her former husband was among those who had been executed. She told her twelve-year-old son 'Your father has died for his country: he did not behave well to us – but now we can think of him with honour.'[3] Within a few months the priest who had attended her husband at his execution told Maud how bravely MacBride had met his death. She wrote to a friend: 'He made a fine and heroic end which has atoned for all. It was a death he had always desired'.[4]

In an RTE interview (Soundings 1979) Seán MacBride recalled how his father's execution had been handled at his school. He said:

I was at school in Paris. I must say I have had tremendous affection for the Jesuits for the way they handled the situation. They were very good because at that time France was fighting Germany, with Britain as an ally. Our Rising was against the British. The Germans were quite close to Paris at the time and you could hear the artillery.

They had a commemoration day every week for the parents of those boys who had been killed and on this day the Director of the school came out and made a most moving speech, explaining that France was at war, in order to protect the liberty of small nations and to ensure that justice was done in the world. He explained that while my father was not fighting on the same side as the French he was fighting for the freedom of a small nation, Ireland, and they all had tremendous sympathy for what the Irish people were trying to do … It was a great way of smoothing things out in the school; as well, all the other boys understood.

Maud was quick to realise the possible future consequences for her family of her husband's execution. She knew that he and the other leaders of the Rising would soon be heroes. By September, Yeats had commemorated them in his poem 'Easter 1916', though he annoyed Maud by his treatment of MacBride's role.

Now that Maud was a widow, Yeats again felt free to propose to her. She told him that there would only be one man in her future life, her son Seán. Yeats turned his attentions to her very attractive daughter Iseult. She too rejected his proposal of marriage in 1917. Writing about Seán at this time, Yeats said: 'The little boy is now quite tall and is going to be very clever and to my amusement has begun to criticise his mother's politics. He has a confident analytical mind and is more like a boy of seventeen than thirteen.'[5]

Though Maud was now only too eager to use the name of her dead husband to assist her own nationalist career, and that of her son in subsequent years, she actively discouraged commemoration of Major John MacBride. It was left to the people of his native area to keep his memory alive. This task was taken up latterly by Eoghan Hughes of Westport.

3

Revolutionary Ireland

Maud MacBride wanted to return to Dublin as soon as possible to be with her nationalist colleagues who were being interned; but the British authorities did not want her in Ireland. They issued a passport for travel to England with no guarantee that she could travel on to Dublin. She remained in France for the winter of 1916/17, but food and fuel were in very short supply. The following summer was spent again in Normandy, living on produce planted there the previous Easter. In September 1917, she decided not to wait any longer and travelled in hope as far as England. Yeats met her and organised accommodation for the family, but she was denied entry to Ireland. After a few months waiting, in February 1918 Seán and his mother travelled illegally to Dublin. Like her husband before her, she hoped the police would ignore her. She bought a large house at 73 St Stephen's Green. Seán joined Na Fianna, a junior branch of the IRA. His mother for the first time began to call herself Madame Gonne-MacBride.

The police ignored her presence for several months, but the following May, in a large round up of Sinn Féiners, she was arrested. Seán witnessed her arrest at their home and removal in a police wagon. She was taken to Holloway Jail in London while Seán went to boarding school at Mount St Benedict in Gorey, County Wexford. In jail Maud was in the company of her good friends, Constance Markievicz and Kathleen Clarke. During her five months in prison, her health deteriorated drastically. There too, she heard of the deaths in France of Lucien Millevoye and her dear sister Kathleen. After some frantic intervention by Yeats and others, she was released into Iseult's custody in 1918, on condition that she did not return to Ireland. Maud took over Yeats's apartment, while he moved to her house in Dublin with his new wife. Seán joined his mother in London where he was tutored by Ezra Pound. Pound wrote to an Irish American friend of Maud's, John Quinn, 'Seán was quite intelligent when she brought him from France but the Troubles in Ireland have ruined his mind and left him, as might be expected at his age, doomed to political futilities...'.[1] Iseult and Pound had become lovers during the period Maud spent in Holloway.[2]

John Quinn was a wealthy Irish-American bachelor who was a patron of the arts. He first met Maud in October 1905 at George Russell's (AE's) house in Dublin in the company of Count and Countess Markievicz, J.M. Synge, Oliver Gogarty and Padraig Colum. This was the start of a long friendship, which included his trying to obtain defamatory evidence in New York against her husband, prior to the pending divorce case. Quinn backed Maud's career financially until his death in 1924.

The 1918 general election in Ireland returned a large Sinn Féin majority. Many of those elected were friends and colleagues of Maud's. As soon as her health had recovered sufficiently in 1919, she, Iseult and Seán travelled to Ireland. The British had banned the Sinn Féin Parliament or Dáil, and the Anglo-Irish war had begun. Seán MacBride, despite his age, became a full member of the IRA. He was assigned to the third battalion of the Dublin Brigade, which covered the area just south of the city centre, from Brunswick Street up to Earlsfort Terrace. He took part in many attacks on British forces, shooting or throwing bombs at patrols before scurrying to safety. Many years later, Seán told his secretary, Louie Coghlan O'Brien that when he first presented himself for membership of the IRA, he went dressed in a grey corduroy and velvet suit, with a yellow waistcoat.

One dark September night in 1920 the military stopped a car at midnight on Rathmines Road in Dublin. The three occupants were ordered out at gunpoint, and were asked for identification. The two passengers, a man and a woman, gave their names as Constance Markievicz and Maurice Bourgeois. She was a member of the banned Dáil, then trying to establish itself as a provisional government. The man was an emissary from the French government. Their driver was the sixteen-year-old Seán MacBride. All three were arrested and taken to the adjacent military barracks. Constance Markievicz was sentenced to two years in jail by a military court for activities relating to her founding of Na Fianna. Bourgeois and MacBride were released after a few days in custody.

The Anglo-Irish war deteriorated. Vicious deeds from one side brought reprisals from the other. The Irish were fighting a guerilla war. The frustrated British military was lashing out on all sides, often against the civilian population. The British would not honour their enemy by calling it a guerilla war. Rather as Lord Curzon, the Foreign Secretary, speaking in the House of Lords in October 1920 said, 'It is the warfare of the Red Indian, of the Apache.' He outlined the state of the country:

> What is going on in Ireland at the present moment? You have there a desperate, a malignant conspiracy known by the name of Sinn Féin, which is endeavouring by every means in its power, seldom fair, usually foul, to sever the connection with this country and to set up an Independent Republic in Ireland. They first tried to effect this end by open rebellion in April, 1916. That attempt ended in failure, and is, I think, not likely to be repeated. They have now passed to a different method of attack — firstly by passive resistance... and secondly, they pursue what I will not honour by describing as guerilla warfare. It is not guerilla warfare. It is the warfare of the Red Indian, of the Apache....[3]

Maud Gonne MacBride had been upset to discover that her son was driving for the IRA. But worse was to follow, the next month, when she found out by accident that he was a full member of that organisation.

One peaceful Sunday afternoon at their home on St Stephen's Green, a shot rang out from an upstairs bedroom. Seán had been cleaning his rifle and had accidentally discharged a round. His mother was horror-stricken, incredulous that he could have been given charge of such a weapon, let alone be expected to use it. As was his custom, he allowed his mother to rail against his superiors in the IRA, his own foolishness, and any other target she wished to attack. Then quietly, by force of reasoned argument, he spoke with her and put his own point of view.

She was not open to such discussion; she was his mother, not his commanding officer. Maud was not interested in tactics or strategy. She did not want to lose him. He told her he did not want to lose her either, yet she was always exposing herself to danger. He told her he understood how she felt, and promised to be more careful; but his duty was clear and he would not shirk it. Maud became tense and fretful every time he left the house, but gradually she accepted his position and began to pray for his safety.

The war in Munster was slipping out of the control of the British army. In Cork the Flying Columns of the IRA, under Tom Barry, were successfully carrying out ambushes in the countryside. The Auxiliaries retaliated by burning much of Cork city. Lord French, the Lord Lieutenant-General, proclaimed martial law in the counties of Cork, Tipperary, Kerry and Limerick. He instanced the 'prevalent and repeated murderous attacks ... upon members of His Majesty's Forces culminating in the ambush, massacre, and mutilation with axes, of sixteen Cadets of the Auxiliary Division, all of whom had served in the late War'.

The same month of December saw the British government introduce the Government of Ireland Act 1920. This Act was the British response to the chaos in Ireland, north and south. It established two Parliaments in Ireland and created partition. It listed the counties of Antrim, Armagh, Down, Fermanagh, Londonderry and Tyrone as comprising Northern Ireland. Thus was the country split without any say by Irish nationalists and with little enthusiasm from the northern unionists. Ireland was partitioned by an Act of the British Parliament, as Seán MacBride was to reiterate for the rest of his life.

4

Anglo-Irish Treaty

The MacBride household was a well-to-do one. It always had servants. Maud liked having plenty of people around her. Another domestic event that caused much consternation occurred when in 1920 Iseult ran off to England with a boy eight years her junior. Seán and Iseult had a very good relationship, each respecting the other's personality and different temperament. He was a traditionalist, a logical person. Iseult was the exact opposite.

Maud, having found respectability for herself and her son, did not intend to let her daughter visit any scandal on the family. She repatriated the young couple and insisted that they marry. Iseult's husband, Francis Stuart, did not get on well with his mother-in-law. Much acrimony occurred between them at St Stephen's Green. Francis Stuart was a poet. He impressed W.B. Yeats, who encouraged him. Stuart was upset to find both Iseult and Maud refer disparingly to his mentor. Though Stuart espoused the republican cause himself, the extremism of his mother-in-law did not endear her to him. His marriage to Iseult was to be fraught with difficulties.

The war continued its brutal way with neither side giving any quarter. In February 1921 Eamon de Valera, the president of Sinn Féin, sent an open letter to members of the House of Commons outlining what the British government forces were perpetrating in Ireland:

> Lest on a plea of ignorance you should disclaim responsibility for what is being done in your name, speaking for the Elected Representatives of the People of Ireland, I now

bring directly to your notice the following facts —

> The troops in Ireland employed by your Government are not only waging an unjust war in a manner contrary to all rules of civilised warfare. In defiance of these rules your forces are guilty of torture, assassination, murder, assaults on women, pillage and looting.[1]

The atrocities were widely publicised. A propaganda war ensued, particularly in the United States, and the British went on the defensive. De Valera went to America on a major fundraising tour on behalf of the provisional government and spent the rest of the War of Independence there. An American commission of inquiry held public hearings in Washington on conditions in Ireland. It concluded that: 'In spite of the British "terror", the majority of the Irish people sanctioned by ballot the Irish Republic, give their allegiance to it, pay taxes to it: and respect the decisions of its courts [Maud Gonne-MacBride acted as a judge in the Sinn Féin courts] and of its civil officials'.[2]

The British government came under intense international pressure to enter into negotiations with the rebels. On 22 June 1921 King George V went to Belfast to open the new Northern Ireland Parliament. He said:

> I have come in person, as the Head of the Empire, to inaugurate this Parliament on Irish soil.... This is a great and critical occasion in the history of the Six Counties, but not for the Six Counties alone, for everything which interests them touches Ireland, and everything which touches Ireland, finds an echo in the remotest parts of the Empire.... The eyes of the whole Empire are on Ireland today.... It is my earnest desire that in Southern Ireland too, there may ere long take place a parallel, to what is now passing in this Hall.... The future lies in the hands of My Irish people themselves.
>
> May this historic gathering be the prelude of a day in which the Irish people, North and South, under one Parliament or two, as those Parliaments may themselves decide, shall work together in common love for Ireland.[3]

A few days later David Lloyd George, the British Prime Minister, proposed a conference between himself and the representatives of Northern Ireland and Southern Ireland, to 'explore to the utmost the possibility of a settlement'. Sir James Craig, the Northern Ireland Prime Minister, refused to meet de Valera as a preliminary to meeting Lloyd George. A truce was agreed in the Anglo-Irish War in July 1921. De Valera travelled to London to meet Lloyd George, who offered the South Dominion status, with Northern Ireland remaining part of the United Kingdom. De Valera knew that this would be unacceptable to those who had fought the British in Ireland, and rejected it. A correspondence between the two men began, but it got nowhere. Finally Lloyd George proposed a conference in London in October: 'The proposals which we have already made have been taken by the whole world as proof that our endeavours for reconciliation and settlement are no empty formula'. De Valera accepted the conference idea and prepared for it.

The IRA was jubilant. It had thwarted the might of the British army to pacify the country. Celebrations were held throughout the South because most people felt that the war would not be resumed. They believed they were on the way to an Irish Republic. But in the North it was different. In Belfast, the day before the truce, many Catholics were murdered and hundreds of their homes were burned. The unionists were fearful of being dominated or taken over by the South.

The MacBride family was glad of the truce that summer. It gave Maud the opportunity to take her children to the Continent. The German economy had been shattered after the war, and the exchange rate for sterling was very favourable for visitors. The family travelled to Bayreuth in Bavaria where they delighted in Wagnerian opera. 'They arrived in Munich in late August and after a few days, Seán left for Dublin. He had been there to buy guns which he hid in a recess cut into books, and posted to a safe address in Ireland'.[4] While they were there, Seán had been summoned back to Dublin. Michael Collins wanted him to go to London as a bodyguard for the Irish delegation at the negotiations.

It was obvious to many perceptive people that the partition of Ireland was a fact and that it would remain so for the foreseeable future. In effect, the forthcoming conference was going to be about the government of the twenty-six counties and its relationship with Britain. This was not what Irish nationalists had struggled for during the 1916 Rising and the Anglo-Irish War. But it was the realpolitik of the situation. De Valera was foremost among those who realised this. He had spent most of the Anglo-Irish War in the United States. On his return, he found that the man who had been in the forefront of the War of Independence, Michael Collins, had become his main challenger for the leadership of Sinn Féin. A hostile power struggle ensued. Eamon de Valera surprised everybody by announcing that he would not lead the Irish delegation at the London conference. Instead, he nominated five envoys and Dáil Eireann gave them written authorisation to negotiate and conclude a treaty of settlement between Ireland and the British Commonwealth. Before final decisions would be made, the cabinet in Dublin was to be consulted. Any draft treaty text was also to be sent to Dublin and a reply awaited.

The envoy plenipotentaries were Arthur Griffith, as Chairman, Michael Collins, Robert Barton, Edmund Duggan and George Gavan Duffy.

5

Civil War

Seán MacBride travelled to London with the Irish delegation
as an aide-de-camp and bodyguard to Michael Collins. His
mother was very proud of her son, but also nervous of the
possibility that, if the talks did not go well, he might be
arrested. If the War did resume, he would be well-known to
the British. MacBride enjoyed returning to London, but was
aware of the physical danger for the delegation. A state of war
still existed and could recommence at any time. The delegation
was also fearful that any of the plenipotentaries might be
interfered with. MacBride's military prowess had come to
Collins's notice. The negotiations dragged on for three months.
MacBride found two distinct groups of people among the
delegation. The military types were rough, tough, working-
class folk. They lodged at Cadogan Square. The others were
the politicians, a higher class who stayed at Hans Place.

MacBride could see that the military despised the politicians.
Collins shared their opinions and lodged with the IRA group,
though, in effect, he was the co-political leader of the delegation.
Not for the first time nor the last, MacBride found himself in
strange circumstances. He was the social equal of the politicians, but he was an army man. He was often in Hans Place
playing chess or bridge, but when he returned to Cadogan
Square, his army colleagues would mock his pretentiousness
in associating with the politicians. MacBride admired Collins,
but was worried by a lot of the British high society attention
he drew on himself. Collins became particularly friendly with
Hazel Lavery, the American-born wife of Sir John Lavery, the
noted portraitist.

The conference lasted for three months, almost collapsing on several occasions. Although the Irish faced the most formidable team the British could muster, de Valera stayed in Dublin.

One day at Hans Place MacBride was playing bridge when Collins arrived in a very angry mood. He upbraided George Gavan Duffy for being involved in such a frivolous matter as a card game while an IRA arms shipment was under threat in Germany. The IRA leader in Germany had attracted the attention of the German police and Collins was worried that they were about to lose the shipment. He ordered MacBride to go at once to Hamburg to attend to the matter, which he did successfully.[1]

In December 1921 the British put a final document on the table entitled *Articles of Agreement for a Treaty between Great Britain and Ireland*. Lloyd George issued an ultimatum to the Irish delegation to sign, or else face the threat of 'immediate and terrible war'. They all signed on 6 December. The twenty-six counties, as Lloyd George had earlier assured de Valera, got Dominion status, with a 'Parliament to make laws for the peace, order and good government of Ireland and an Executive responsible to that Parliament and shall be known as the Irish Free State'. The Members of the Irish Parliament would take an oath to the British monarch, and the Irish Free State would be a member of the British Commonwealth. A commission would delineate the boundary with Northern Ireland, 'in accordance with the wishes of the inhabitants, so far as may be compatible with economic and geographic conditions'.

The terms of the Treaty split the country. Many felt that, under the circumstances, it was as good as could be expected. They argued, like Collins, that it could prove to be a stepping stone towards the achievement of their ultimate aim, a thirty-two county republic. Arthur Griffith fully realised the enormity of what had been achieved for the twenty-six counties.

But de Valera rejected the Treaty and sought to introduce an alternative to it called 'Document Number Two', giving Ireland an 'External Association with Britain and the Commonwealth'. Others rejected any notion of compromise on a fully independent thirty-two county republic. The IRA was split on the issue.

During December, the Dáil debated the terms of the Treaty in Earlsfort Terrace. It was a bitter and divisive exercise, mirroring the schism in the country. The main point of contention probably was the inclusion of the oath to the sovereign. The fact of partition seemed to be a matter that could be resolved later.

Around the corner from Earlsfort Terrace, at the MacBride home, there was also deep division. Maud MacBride had come through many bitter experiences in her long love affair with nationalist Ireland. The horrors of war were forever etched on her mind. The people, she saw, wanted peace. She believed that the Treaty would afford possibilities to build on. It could be a stepping stone, but no more than that, she said. Her young, though experienced son, disagreed vigorously with her, denouncing the Treaty as a sellout to the men of 1916 and the IRA who had stymied the brutal tactics of the British army. His attitude was that they had come this far militarily and were not going to turn back. He knew the intentions of many in the army because he had recently been promoted to assistant director of organisation to Ernie O'Malley.

O'Malley was a native of Castlebar, whose family had moved to Dublin while he was still a youth. Major John MacBride knew the O'Malleys well and was a frequent visitor to their Dublin home. Despite the bitter words that had been spoken and written about Major John, by the poets Yeats and Tom Kettle, Ernie O'Malley had nothing but good memories of the Major. This would have made his close association with Seán MacBride initially sensitive. Seán had no memories of his father save the bitter words he had heard from his mother. But Seán never spoke of his late father. O'Malley had been a medical student at the time of the 1916 Rising and had joined in the fighting. He felt great resentment when the executions began, but when MacBride was executed, that was replaced by a 'strange rage'. As he wrote, 'I had known MacBride; he had been in our house a week before the Rising' and laughed when O'Malley had told him that he intended to join the British army. MacBride, giving little away, merely said, 'No, you won't'. O'Malley recalled the Major's kind personality when he wrote, 'he had been kind to us as children: he would leave the other visitors, to talk to us. With him we dropped our

best company manners and felt at ease'.[2] The Major regaled
the children with stories of his exploits, particularly those of
the Boer War.

Seán's mother believed that there was a good possibility
that the Treaty might be passed. The IRB, which Collins controlled, had not taken a public stance against it, though she
did know that the six female TDs were going to vote against
it in the Dáil.

The crucial vote was taken in early January 1922. The
Treaty was accepted by sixty-four votes to fifty-seven. Eamon
de Valera resigned as president of the Dáil and was replaced
by Arthur Griffith. That same month an Irish Race Convention
was held in Paris. Seventeen countries were represented to
discuss Irish culture and consider how best Ireland could be
helped in the present situation. The Irish delegation was
composed of people from various political, religious and cultural
backgrounds. The new divisions were well-mirrored in Paris,
with Maud Gonne MacBride a delegate from the new provisional government and her friend Constance Markievicz
representing those who had voted against the Treaty.
W.B. Yeats and Douglas Hyde also attended.

The new provisional government proceeded to try to take
over from the departing British. The anti-Treaty section of
the IRA refused to recognise the new government or its writ
and resented efforts by the government to set up its own army
and police force. Armed conflict between the two groups
became inevitable. Both sides began to compete in occupying
installations vacated by the British.

The IRA in Dublin took over and fortified the large Four
Courts complex beside the river Liffey on 14 April 1922. This
was the most blatant and obvious sign of its unwillingness to
accept the new state's institutions. Among the men who
began to garrison the Four Courts was Seán MacBride. He
had just finished a three month period as secretary to de
Valera after the vote on the Treaty.

The IRA decided to call a meeting of its ruling body at the
Mansion House on 18 June — an army convention — to try to
resolve the deteriorating situation. Many of its members had
joined the new state army. The provisional government ordered
that none of its soldiers attend, but the army convention went

ahead. It set up a new IRA executive and a fresh organisational structure, neither of which recognised the government or its army. The new IRA began to exert itself around the country and hostilities occurred, though on a small scale.

One motion before the Mansion house convention had urged an attack on the remaining British military presence. When this was voted down, MacBride jumped up shouting in his strange French-accented voice, swinging over his head his .45 Colt automatic, at the end of a lanyard, 'All who are in favour of the Republic follow me to the Four Courts'.[3]

A general election was to be held in June 1922. Michael Collins and de Valera agreed that the two sections of Sinn Féin would be allocated the same proportion of seats after the election as they held before it. This was to avoid open warfare during the election campaign. Collins signed a peace agreement with the Northern Ireland government, but he then colluded with the IRA in launching cross-border attacks against the North's security forces. Collins had maintained close connections with the IRA within the Four Courts, though the troops were there in defiance of the government. As Seán MacBride had seen in London, Collins had much more in common with the army than with the politicians.

The result of the general election to the Third Dáil in June 1922 caused even more bitterness. Despite the Collins-de Valera election pact, the results were: pro-Treaty 58 TDs, anti-Treaty, 36 TDs. Labour got 17 seats, Farmers 7 and Independents 10. Collins was immediately accused of reneging on the pact.

The IRA realised that it was fast losing control of the situation. Its members would have to make a stand against the new government, but what precisely they should do was not clear.

There were several female republicans in the Four Courts. Among them was a twenty-one-year-old named Catalina (Kid) Bulfin, whose father William, had been a writer and friend of Arthur Griffith. Bulfin had emigrated to Argentina when he was twenty. There he owned and edited an Irish newspaper — *Southern Cross*. He later returned home and published *Rambles in Erin*. Both his son, Eamon, and Catalina were born in Buenos Aires. She and Seán became friends.

All of the women in the movement were accepted as equals by the men and frequently carried guns.

During the early part of the occupation of the Four Courts, life there was fairly casual. In the first volume of his autobiography, C.S. Andrews wrote: 'Almost every morning Ernie O'Malley and Seán MacBride would stroll up Grafton Street where they would meet some College girls for coffee in Mitchells or Roberts Cafes'. Andrews says that 'due to his parents he [MacBride] was treated by everyone with a diffidence', though this was 'disassociated from his personal qualities, the principal one was his charm'.[4] Andrews regarded MacBride as a boy on a man's errand. He also recalled how, one Sunday, O'Malley, MacBride and himself 'commandeered a car from some harmless citizen to go for a drive in the country', where they accidentally met de Valera who was very friendly. Andrews also recalled another occasion in Nassau Street, when they crashed into an army lorry, 'MacBride jumped out, flourishing his .45 Colt', before they made their escape into the crowd. Ernie O'Malley later wrote of the Four courts, 'Liam Mellows, the Quartermaster General, endeavoured to import arms. Officers were sent to foreign countries. Seán MacBride, the Assistant Director of Operations, a native French speaker, departed on mysterious journies. Small quantities of arms arrived'.[5]

An event occurred on 22 June which was to make the British demand action against those occupying the Four Courts. Field-Marshall Sir Henry Wilson was assassinated in London. Though born in Longford, Wilson espoused the Ulster Unionist cause and actively encouraged Lloyd George to greater coercion in Ireland. The murder provided the British government with an opportunity it wanted to press the Irish government to move against the IRA in the Four Courts. The British were well aware of Collins's fellow feelings for the IRA. Lloyd George sent a stern letter to Collins about the continuation of the IRA presence in the Four Courts:

Dear Mr. Collins, I am desired by His Majesty's Government to inform you that documents have been found upon the murderers of Sir Henry Wilson which clearly connect the assassins with the Irish Republican Army, and which further reveal the existence of a definite conspiracy against the peace and order of this country. Other information has reached His Majesty's Government showing that active preparations are on foot among the irregular elements of the I.R.A. to resume attacks upon the lives and property of British subjects both in England and in Ulster. The ambiguous position of the Irish Republican Army can no longer be ignored by the British Government. Still less can Mr. Rory O'Connor be permitted to remain with his followers and his arsenal in open rebellion in the heart of Dublin in possession of the Courts of Justice, organising and sending out from this centre enterprises of murder not only in the area of your Government but also in the six Northern Counties and in Great Britain. His Majesty's Government cannot consent to a continuance of this state of things, and they feel entitled to ask you formally to bring it to an end forthwith. Assistance has on various occasions been given to Dominions of the Empire in cases where their authority was challenged by rebellion on their soil; and His Majesty's Government are prepared to place at your disposal the necessary pieces of artillery which may be required, or otherwise to assist you as may be arranged. I am to inform you that they regard the continued toleration of this rebellious defiance of principles of the Treaty as incompatible with its faithful execution. They feel that now you are supported by the declared will of the Irish people in favour of the Treaty, they have a right to expect that the necessary action will be taken by your Government without delay.[6]

On 26 June 1922 the Free State army arrested a Four Courts officer. Ernie O'Malley and Seán MacBride retaliated by arresting Ginger O'Connell, a Lieutenant General of the Free State army. The IRA thought that this might be the spark that would start a conflagration and so began to prepare for an offensive.

While Seán MacBride was in the Four Courts, his mother went again to Paris, on behalf of the government. Because of her long and close relationship with Arthur Griffith, he had asked her to go there to publicise the efforts being made to establish the new state. It was work she had long lived for.

Like everyone else, she was concerned about the tussle between the IRA and the government. On 29 June she read in the French press that the Free State army was shelling the Four Courts with guns loaned by the British. Maud Gonne MacBride could think of nothing except the safety of her son. She rushed back to Dublin and sought to organise a group of women to act as intermediaries between the opposing forces.

But the Four Courts was in ruins and its garrison of nearly 200 men had surrendered. All were taken to Mountjoy Jail. Maud did not see her son. The women, including Kid Bulfin, were placed in Kilmainham jail. Everybody knew this was certainly the start of the long expected Civil War. Because of this, Maud and her group of women persisted in trying to mediate between the government and the IRA. At that stage the government was living permanently at Government Buildings in Upper Merrion Street, under constant guard. They were desperately trying to keep the fledgeling state afloat and avoid chaos and a return of the British. Griffith did not want to meet his old friend under such circumstances, but she insisted. Collins, Griffith and Cosgrave met the women and explained that the IRA would have to lay down their arms and recognise the legitimate government.

The strain on the three men was obvious, with Griffith in the worst state. 'We are a Government now and we have to keep order', he told Maud MacBride, whose proposal was that both sides should lay their arms aside and let the Dáil settle the matter peacefully. Within six weeks, on 12 August 1922, Griffith was dead, dying under an assumed name (for security reasons) in St Vincent's Hospital. He had been Maud MacBride's main link with the Free State. Now, with her son still incarcerated and the Civil War reaching appalling proportions in the countryside, she decided henceforth to support the republican anti-Treaty side. Her home in St Stephen's Green became a centre for their casualties and a safe house for republicans on the run.

The Free State army was better equipped than the IRA because of assistance from the British. It succeeded in pushing the IRA southwards and forcing it into guerilla tactics. Ten days after Griffith's death, Michael Collins was killed in an ambush in County Cork. The Free State's two most prominent leaders were dead. Now the government was in the hands of William Cosgrave who was shortly to be President of the Executive Council, Kevin O'Higgins the Minister for Justice and the Minister for Defence, Richard Mulcahy. They faced a terrifying prospect.

6

IRA Activist

The new Parliament convened at the Royal Dublin Society, Leinster Lawn, Kildare Street on 9 September 1922. William Cosgrave said: 'We are the custodians of the rights of the people and we shall not hesitate to shoulder them. We are willing to come to a peaceful understanding with those in arms, but it must be on a definite basis. We want peace with England on the terms agreed to by the country. We are satisfied that the nation stands to lose incomparably less from the armed internal opposition than from a reconquest. The National Army is prepared to pay its price, and so are we.'[1]

The anti-Treaty TDs did not take their seats in the Dáil and did not recognise its legitimacy, claiming that the Second Dáil only could be recognised. De Valera, who was active with the IRA in Munster, wrote a long letter to Frank Aiken, the IRA chief of staff, and members of its executive about setting up an alternative 'Government for the Republic', which might have to accept the status quo with the United Kingdom. It was another example of de Valera's convoluted thinking, as he sought a compromise way out of the political impasse. The Catholic bishops condemned the IRA campaign, but it made little difference to the continuing viciousness of the Civil War.

Madame MacBride's son-in-law, Francis Stuart, was jailed in Mountjoy along with Seán. She tried to organise help for the ever increasing number of prisoners, but was refused entry to the prison. The authorities were giving no information on the whereabouts or condition of any prisoner.

A new constitution was introduced in early December. Military courts were established to hear cases and hand down summary justice. Several executions of IRA men were carried out. The IRA retaliated by shooting dead one of the Dáil deputies, Seán Hales, and wounding another, Pádraig Ó Máille. The government felt that its existence was under direct and immediate threat. It knew the majority of the citizens and all the major institutions supported it and so determined to take drastic action.

Several leaders of the IRA, captured after the surrender of the Four Courts, along with hundreds of other volunteers, were still in Mountjoy. Among the leaders were some who had signed the IRA proclamation at the beginning of the Civil War: Liam Mellows, Rory O'Connor and Joseph McKelvey. Seán MacBride shared a cell with Rory O'Connor. In the early morning of 8 December, O'Connor and MacBride were both awakened and told to dress. They were taken through the prison to a special holding area. MacBride was soon brought back alone to his cell. The next morning at Mass, MacBride heard that O'Connor, Mellows, McKelvey and Dick Barret had been shot, as a reprisal for the murder of the Dáil deputy. Rory O'Connor had been the best man at the wedding of Kevin O'Higgins, the Minister of Justice, who had sanctioned the executions.

After the Mass, MacBride accosted the priest to tell him of the injustice of what had occurred. The priest was on his way out of the prison as MacBride walked along with him in intense discussion. Without knowing quite what he was doing, he found himself outside the prison walls. For whatever reason, he bade the priest 'goodbye' and returned to Mountjoy.

The executions stunned the country. That same day in Dáil Eireann, Thomas Johnston, the Leader of the Labour Party, summed up the feelings of many when he said: 'The four men in Mountjoy have been in your charge for five months. You were charged with the care of these men; that was your duty as guardians of the law. You could have charged them with an offence. You held them as a defence, and your duty was to care for them... The Government of Saorstát Eireann announces apparently with pride that they have taken out four men, and as a reprisal for that assassination, murdered them'.[2]

Madame MacBride feared for the lives of the other prisoners, particularly her son and son-in-law, and protested outside the gates of the prison. She and Charlotte Despard, a radical socialist and feminist, founded the Women's Prisoners Defence League (WPDL) at a meeting in the Mansion House. This group, dubbed 'The Mothers', kept up a constant harassment of the government, holding a march and a meeting in O'Connell Street every Sunday. The authorities responded by breaking up the gatherings. They also began a series of raids on Maud MacBride's house, destroying much valuable documentary material. She and Charlotte Despard moved out of the city to Roebuck House in Clonskeagh, where they established a field hospital and refuge for republican activists. Maud MacBride was arrested twice. The first time she spent just one night in jail, but on the second occasion in January 1923 she joined a hunger strike with other women in Kilmainham Jail. She remained on strike for twenty days until, at the intervention of W.B. Yeats, she was released.

The Civil War continued, but it was obvious that the IRA was being defeated. The government executed 77 republicans between November 1922 and May 1923. In April 1923, de Valera and Frank Aiken ordered a suspension of all IRA activity. De Valera proclaimed:

Soldiers of Liberty! Legion of the Rearguard! The Republic can no longer be defended successfully by your arms. Further sacrifice of life would now be vain, and your continuance of the struggle in arms unwise in the national interest.

Military victory must be allowed to rest for the moment with those who have destroyed the Republic. Other means must be sought to safeguard the nation's rights.[3]

The Cosgrave administration continued to try to exercise its duties and called a general election for August 1923. The government was now formed into a party named Cumann na nGaedhal. Sinn Féin, under Eamon de Valera, contested the election on an abstentionist basis. During the campaign de Valera was arrested and interned. Many prisoners became Sinn Féin candidates. The result was Cumann na nGaedhal 63 seats, Sinn Féin Republicans 44, Labour 14, Farmers 15, Others 15 seats. It was a 'satisfactory' result for all sides. The 'republicans' still maintained their own 'government' and the IRA's General Headquarters was under the control of Frank Aiken.

Inside the jails, prisoners were going on hunger strike. Outside, Madame MacBride and the WDPL continued to highlight the internment of republicans. Soon, after a few deaths occurred, the strikes ended and the government began to experiment with selective releases. In December 1923, to relieve congestion in Mountjoy, the authorities began to transfer some prisoners to Kilmainham. This was done by ambulance in the early hours of the morning. On one such trip when Seán MacBride and Michael Price were in the ambulance, the driver lost his way. The guard went to consult with the driver. MacBride and Price jumped out and ran. They were later stopped by soldiers but were allowed to continue.

The two men split up and MacBride made his way through back gardens to the house of people he knew. He knocked loudly on the door. A figure appeared at the upstairs window to see a man lurking in the garden. A window was opened and MacBride announced who he was. He was told that Seán MacBride was in Mountjoy. 'But I've just escaped!' MacBride pleaded in the cold and dark, 'I've got to get a safe house.' Still the occupant would not come down to see him up close. These were dangerous times and you could be shot for harbouring a fugitive. 'Ask me a question about something I should know if I am who I say I am', MacBride said. He responded favourably to his questioner, who then rushed downstairs, welcomed him in and fed him. MacBride remained there in hiding for three days until the search had been scaled down. Then he made his way to Roebuck House to see his mother. He was welcomed warmly. He was amazed to see the workshops his mother had established to give employment to released prisoners. She told him that the government was refusing to employ any former IRA people, almost encouraging them to emigrate. Francis Stuart was among those who had been released and he went to live at Roebuck House with Iseult.

Seán MacBride was now assigned to the headquarters staff of the IRA where he was to remain for almost fifteen years though always on the run. Most IRA men were interested in getting out of jail, finding a job, trying to start a normal life in the state that was clearly going to survive for the foreseeable future. The government was taking no chances and suspended habeus corpus for the duration of 1924.

Towards the end of 1924 MacBride was involved in a daring plan to rescue escaping internees from the beach at Larne in County Antrim. Frank Aiken appointed him officer in charge. Taking three colleagues with him, Tom Heavy and Tony Woods whom he knew well, and Frank Barry a seaman, they went to Belfast. At the docks MacBride under the assumed name of Lt Swift of the Royal Navy, paid £200 for an ex-Canadian ML boat. He named it the St George, a name he felt would not arouse suspicion in the security-conscious Belfast shipyards. The IRA had been told that a group of internees at Larne were tunnelling towards the beach. They requested a boat to pick them up as they escaped. A local Belfast woman named Frances Brady, was their go-between with MacBride's group. The latter had to live on the boat for several weeks while its engines were being overhauled. They aroused no suspicion and on completion of the work, they had a drinks party for the local harbourmaster, which included toasting the King. Then word came that the tunnel at Larne had been discovered and it was unclear whether any of the prisoners had escaped. MacBride decided to sail to Larne and check the beach. But at Bangor he was informed that no prisoners had escaped. MacBride then decided to sail the boat, in which the IRA had made a major investment, to Dun Laoire. Off Newcastle, in Dundrum Bay, the boat developed engine trouble. They dropped anchor to try to fix it. That night a storm blew up and beached the boat near the golf links. The local coastguard rescued all four of them. The three crew were put up in a local hotel. MacBride was taken to the Ballykinlar army camp where he spent several days as a guest of the Queen's Own Royal West Kent regiment. In the meantime the crew took it in turns to stay aboard the boat, to stop locals claiming salvage rights. After a period of a few weeks it became apparent that they would not be able to refloat the boat. The incident was reported in the Belfast and Dublin papers. The correct names of the three crew were given. These were readily identifiable as IRA men to the Dublin police. But the Northern authorities remained unsuspicious. Gradually the four returned to Dublin, though after the Christmas holiday MacBride returned for an inquiry into the accident. After Easter he went north again for a court case in which a local man was claiming salvage rights over the St George. MacBride spoke eloquently and won the case, all the while passing himself off as Lt Swift of the Royal Navy.[4]

MacBride worked again for de Valera for a short period as his personal secretary. Early in 1925 they both travelled to Rome to meet Archbishop Mannix of Melbourne and Monsignor John Hagan, Rector of the Irish College, and an ardent Irish nationalist. Mannix was a native of Cork and had gone to Melbourne in 1912. There he had become an ardent advocate of Irish nationalism, leading a successful campaign in Australia to fight overseas con-scription in the Great War. He visited the United States in 1920 where he met and was impressed with de Valera. According to MacBride, Mannix strongly advised de Valera to enter Dáil Eireann. MacBride believed that such advice was what de Valera wanted to hear from this eminent Irish Churchman.[5]

MacBride was a very busy man between his IRA duties, his legal studies at University College, Dublin, and his courtship of Kid Bulfin. She was a very stylish 'Twenties' young woman, whose flat in Dublin attracted many admirers. Seán's mother admired her spirit and was hopeful that they would marry. Kid Bulfin was described by C.S. Andrews thus: 'Kid Bulfin, who was the youngest and most sophisticated of them, had read unusually extensively. She was a typical woman of the Twenties, elegant, smoking cigarettes through a very long holder, short-skirted and not sparing décolletage.' In the same book, Andrews describes MacBride:

He was brought up in situations where he only met the important people in the Independence movement. He behaved from boyhood as if he was one of them. He was accepted as such by everyone he met. A tall man, with thin nondescript hair, his features were finely wrought, but his hollow cheeks and deep set haunted eyes gave him something of the appearance of a character in a Gothic novel. He spoke ... in a peculiarly soothing manner. He was extremely brave and had an aristocratic indifference to money. On the question of Separation MacBride never lost the Fenian faith.[6]

Kid Bulfin had been jailed for one year in Kilmainham after the capture of the Four Courts. She was as dedicated to the national cause as Seán. From the time they met in the Four Courts, they had kept in touch with each other. When he escaped and got a post in the headquarters of the IRA, she became his secretary. Their friends did not believe it when they told them that they intended to get married. He was not quite twenty-one, though she was four years older. Most of their contemporaries could not afford such a step.

On Seán's twenty-first birthday in January 1925 he and Kid Bulfin were married at University Church on St Stephen's Green, just a few doors away from his former home. The ceremony had to be a surreptitious affair because he was a senior IRA figure, still on the run from the security forces. He slept in a safe house in Sandymount the night before his wedding, sharing a bed with two friends. He had arranged with an ex-prisoner colleague of his, whose father owned a garage, to collect him in the morning and drive him to the church. This man knew MacBride to be a practical joker and assumed that the announced marriage was a joke. He did not show up with the car. So MacBride and his best man, a Kerryman called Tom Daly, had to walk to the church, arriving forty-five minutes late. Kid Bulfin was waiting patiently.

The couple, with the active encouragement of Madame MacBride, left for the Continent where they could live in safety, after so many years of active service in Ireland. They settled in Paris, where Seán began work as a journalist for the Havas Agency. Later they moved to London where he, under the assumed name of Maguire, worked as a subeditor for the Conservative *Morning Post*. The couple stayed away from Ireland for more than a year until their first child was due, but they kept in touch with the unfolding events at home.

For most of the time Seán lived on his mother's money, though, when asked how did he make ends meet in Paris, he used to say that he got to know a racing syndicate which gave him excellent tips.

7

On the Run

The abstentionist Sinn Féin TDs were at a loss to know what to do. Since they were not sitting in the Dáil, they received no salary. De Valera was determined to break this logjam, but he had little control within the IRA. He realised that military methods were finished. The way forward had to be political, but his problem was to try and bring as many people with him as possible. Gradually, soundings were taken within Sinn Féin about a possible political role within the Free State. The Dáil was running the country and, since Sinn Féin was the second largest elected grouping, some of its supporters thought they should take their seats in the detested parliament.

Within the IRA it was different. Although some senior figures like Frank Aiken and Seán Lemass were becoming increasingly sceptical about the military option, most were not. Among these was Seán MacBride, who, despite his closeness to de Valera, regarded a political role as a sellout. The Army Council discussed it and rejected it. Once more, the less militant men, those who wanted an immediate stake in the country, drifted away from the IRA towards constitutional politics.

The Boundary Commission, upon which many Irish nationalists had pinned hopes for a large transfer of Northern Ireland territory to the Free State, had its report leaked in November 1925. Consternation followed when it became clear that only a small transfer, in both directions, was recommended. The three governments involved met quickly and agreed that there should be no changes at all on the existing border. To ease the blow, the British government agreed to waive a large Irish debt to the British Exchequer. The republicans were furious with this acceptance of the existing border. It demonstrated to them that they had been right all along about the folly of signing a Treaty which could be so readily interpreted. The IRA were strengthened in their belief that they alone would unite Ireland.

The Boundary Agreement was signed on 3 December 1925 by Stanley Baldwin and Winston Churchill for the British government, W.T. Cosgrave, Kevin O'Higgins and Ernest Blythe on behalf of the Irish Free State, and James Craig for the government of Northern Ireland.

Speaking in the Northern Parliament, Craig said: 'From the beginning of the Boundary controversy the Cabinet, the Government, and the people of Ulster have been absolutely united on a policy which today is being consecrated by the Agreement.'

W.T. Cosgrave was quoted on 4 December 1925 as saying:

I firmly believe that we have found the only solution to a very difficult situation to which the representatives of all of the Governments could have subscribed. I believe that the result is a sane and constructive one, and that it will tend to foster cordial relations, a better understanding, and a greater measure of mutual respect and goodwill. It will remove obstacles which have ever been a source of bitter conflict between the peoples of Northern Ireland and the Irish Free State.

I want you to put on record my belief that this solution will tend more surely and more speedily towards bringing about the ultimate political unity of the two sections of the country than any other course which could have been adopted in the circumstances with which we were confronted. The grave problems which we were called on to solve were problems which had been inherited, and which all efforts made up to the present had not succeeded in solving.

It is necessary to point out that the agreement, while perhaps not appearing at the moment to be a complete and satisfactory solution of our problems, will nevertheless contribute more surely to better relations and foster fraternal feelings between England and Ireland than anything hitherto achieved by us. We have all been impressed by the great assistance which has been rendered to us by those helping to bring about a satisfactory compromise, but I must caution our people that it is not to-day or tomorrow, but within two or three months, that we shall begin to realize the benefits of this agreement.[1]

Eamon de Valera felt that the Agreement made it all the more imperative for the Sinn Féin TDs to be in the Dáil, where they could attack the government day by day. The party was by now receiving little financial assistance from the United States and would wither away unless it became politically engaged. A Sinn Féin Ard Fheis was called to discuss the matter in March 1926. Intense canvassing took place on this New Departure.

The Sinn Féin Ard Fheis, called to consider de Valera's plan that Sinn Féin TDs should take their seats in the Dáil, was very divisive. In the end it rejected his idea. He resigned as president and began to organise a new party which would enter the Dáil as soon as the oath of allegiance to the monarch was removed. Another major split in the republican political and army factions took place. In May 1926 the new party — Fianna Fáil — was founded.

Republicans were shocked when the legendary IRA figure, Dan Breen, abstentionist TD for Tipperary, took the oath of allegiance to the King and entered the Dáil in January 1927. An Phoblacht commented: 'Irishmen will regret that he should have overshadowed his other days by this crime'.[2]

A general election was announced for June 1927. Abortive efforts were made to work out an alliance between Sinn Féin-IRA and Fianna Fáil. The election results were: Cumann na nGaedhael 47, Fianna Fáil 44, Labour 22, Farmers 11, National League 8, Sinn Féin 5, Others 15. Because of its lack of funds Sinn Féin could nominate only 15 candidates. Dan Breen lost his seat. De Valera was jubilant with the overall result. Under the constitution, a member of the Dáil could demand a referendum to change the constitution. This de Valera intended to do, campaigning to have the Oath removed. He felt that such a referendum could be won. Fianna Fáil could then enter the Dáil and perhaps take power.

Seán MacBride, with his wife and daughter Anna, returned to Ireland in that same year. They took up residence at Roebuck House with Madame MacBride. The house continued to be a hive of industrial activity in support of republicans. Seán was appointed director of intelligence with the IRA and once more was on the run from the authorities.

Maud and Charlotte Despard had set up a jam factory in the gardens of Roebuck House, to give employment to the mothers and wives of imprisoned republicans. Seán and Kid were handed the management of the factory as a way of earning their living, but Kid was the one who had to do the work. At a later stage, Seán asked the youthful Louie Coughlan, whose older sister May had been imprisoned with Kid in Kilmainham, to join the management team. Louie was then doing a shorthand and book-keeping course at the Gregg School in Grafton Street. Seán persuaded her to continue her studies at night and work at Roebuck during the day. So Kid and Louie ran the factory together, travelling across the city to look for orders for their jam. The Monument Creamery chain of shops was their best customer.

Kid no longer played any role within the IRA or the national movement. She was on the periphery, all the time supporting her husband's various careers, but taking no action on her own initiative.

As the MacBrides were returning home from the Continent, an event occurred which threw the political situation into ferment. The Minister for Justice, Kevin O'Higgins, a figure hated by the republicans for his perceived harshness to them, was assassinated while walking to Mass in Booterstown, County Dublin. Although the IRA, fearing reprisals, publicly denied responsibility, the government arrested large numbers of their members, including MacBride. He was charged with the murder and a witness identified him as one of the assailants. His family feared the worst. Luckily for him, the murder had taken place while he was on his way back to Ireland. He was able to call Senator Bryan Cooper, whom he had spoken to on the boat, as a witness.

MacBride had a sceptical view of positive identification witnesses for the rest of his life. He was acquitted of the murder, but was not released. Instead, he was charged under

the Public Safety Act as a subversive and was interned in
Mountjoy. His mother was furious at the injustice of it all and
once more she found herself activating her WPDL to protest
against the imprisonment. Her hatred of the government
knew no bounds.

Ironically in earlier times as a law student, O'Higgins had
commemorated the death of Major John MacBride in verse:

How He Died

I never was greatly a friend to John MacBride
But he caught my heart in the end by the death he died,
Rich be his sleep and deep
By Kilmainham side!

For when they called him out, the cold last tryst to abide,
The cheeks of some of the men, though their hearts were stout
Had marked the ebb of the tide
And — set your lips as you can —
To riddle a smiling man is not, on the present plan
So perfectly cut and dried,
But it takes a bit of the stiffening out of a soldier's pride!
Then in a cheery voice
As to friends at his side
'Lads' said the rebel 'I know if you had the choice
You'd let the thing abide
For you see, though my hands aren't tied,
I'd be giving away too much it 'twas fighting I tried.
But the business has to be done
Though it isn't good fun.
Let you rest well o' nights; myself will do for one
And tell them nobody cried.

Now some of you decent chaps
Aren't wonderful shots perhaps
But I'm not much farther off than a hop and a stride
So you'll hit with the blessing of God
Or it is odd'
Said the rebel MacBride.

And when they thought anon
Of putting a bandage on
He moved aside —
'No' said John
'There's nothing you need to hide
Right or wrong.
I've drunk my tea pretty strong
And faith! I've stared down life's barrels so long
I can do with the talk of a few of them open-eyed.
Just a moment,' he said,
'Wait till I bow my head, Then you can put me to bed.'
He bowed his head — and then he died.

So while I was never your friend,
Old John MacBride,
You caught my heart in the end
By the death you died;
Deep be the sleep you keep
By Kilmainham's side!

                     K.C.H. (Kevin Christopher Higgins).[3]

The assassination of Kevin O'Higgins and the reaction of the
government made de Valera and his followers attempt to
enter the Dáil without signing the register, the recognised
method of taking the Oath. The Clerk of the Dáil barred their
entry and they withdrew. The government had threatened
emergency legislation which they hoped would force Fianna
Fáil to bury their opposition to the Oath and take their seats.
The government realised that until Fianna Fáil entered the
House, the Dáil would not be a true Parliament. De Valera
sought legal advice, which told him that the Oath was an
empty formula and that they could sign the register merely as
a way of being allowed to take their seats. Fianna Fáil issued
a statement:

> The required declaration is not an oath, that the signing of
> it implies no contractual obligation, and that it has no
> binding significance in law: that in short, it is merely an
> empty political formula which deputies could conscientiously
> sign, without becoming involved in obligations of loyalty to
> the English Crown.[4]

The Fianna Fáil members took their seats and the proposed new legislation was tabled. It resulted in a 71 vote tie. The Speaker supported the government. The Taoiseach, William Cosgrave, called a general election for the next month. Once again Sinn Féin and the IRA were placed in an impossible position with de Valera proving to wavering republicans that, in practice, political methods could produce results. It looked like the end of the Cosgrave regime hated by republicans. Sinn Féin-IRA decided that, tactically, their policy for the election would be to defeat the Cosgrave government. They could not afford to run candidates themselves. The election results were: Cumman na nGaedhal 62, Fianna Fáil 57, Labour 13, Farmers 6, National League 2, Others 13. Cosgrave was re-elected Taoiseach by 76 votes to 70 for de Valera.

8

Saor Eire

Fianna Fáil would have to wait and organise in anticipation of victory in the next election, but the IRA knew that the Cosgrave government would move to obliterate them. They felt they had to attack or else face total defeat. They still hoped for an understanding with their erstwhile colleagues in Fianna Fáil, but, as time went on, it became obvious that only the military diehards and those looking for a left-wing workers' republic remained outside Fianna Fáil. The prisons filled up again and the government treated IRA prisoners harshly. The IRA was desperately under-resourced. Those, like MacBride, who were working at GHQ, were paid little.

Gradually the idea began to take hold that the IRA needed another organisation, to attract republicans who were drawn to Fianna Fáil. A political wing became a constant topic of debate, causing much divisiveness. Sinn Féin was almost moribund. When some members realised that military action would not be forthcoming immediately, they favoured a radical left-wing group, but the IRA Army Council voted it down. Instead, in 1929 they countenanced a loose federation of republican groups in a body called Comhairle na Poblachta. Seán MacBride and his mother both belonged to this organisation. Unlike her, he was doubtful about becoming embroiled in social issues. The authorities became alarmed at the new group and arrested MacBride again. He spent the next five months in jail. During legal proceedings to have him released, he was described as a 'Managing Director of the Family Firm at Roebuck House, involved in a jam making factory and an ornamental emporium'.

The left wingers within the IRA continued to push for a radical departure, especially since Comhairle na Poblachta was used as a device to outflank their demands. They plotted to win approval at the next Army Convention.

On his release, MacBride attended an anti-imperialist conference in Berlin. There he met both Pandit Nehru and Ho Chi Minh. MacBride was again arrested in 1929 in Tralee, County Kerry, while attending an IRA meeting. The police found incriminating papers on him. In a major reversal of judicial practice, the judge, Justice Hanna, held that the police were exceeding their powers by arresting people on mere suspicion and that possession of documents was not enough proof of guilt. MacBride was released and the IRA enjoyed a welcome respite until the government changed the law.

The group within the IRA demanding a move to the left were gradually winning approval. The name of the new movement was Saor Eire. It was launched by Seán MacBride, its chairman, in the Iona Hall in North Great Georges Street, Dublin in 1931. About 150 people avoided police to attend. They heard MacBride, regarded as the IRA's chief theoretician, launch a ferocious attack on the state as a mere 'associated agency' of 'imperial power'. He called on all supporters to rally to the cause of militancy:

In 1916 British rule was exercised nakedly by British officials. Power was in the hands of planters and landlords and their associates in banking and industrial combines. The mass of the Irish people were in bondage to the few and an army and a police force were stationed here to see that the slaves behaved and made their masters rich. The State was the association of rifles and batons, jails, bailiffs and thuggery, with the wealth of the aliens and traitors, to rob and strangle a sovereign people.

Today Dublin Castle, they say, is no more. But the aliens have not been dispossessed: landlordism has not been abolished, and landlords have not been made disgorge; banks, which are the pooling of money stolen from us, have not come under our control; and the machinery of the State is today exactly as in pre-Treaty days — a tyranny associated

with the interests that beggared us. The Free State
Parliament is only an *associated agency* for carrying out the
Imperial purpose, and just as the individual land agent
waxed rich in his master's service, so now an association of
Imperial agents prosper on the ruin of their country and
squabble among themselves for the offices. For we tell you
choice of government for the State is nothing except choice
of agents for the class that enslave us. Good or bad government means what the good or bad agent meant in other
days, and good men in office no more means the end of
slavery than a good agent meant the end of landlordism.

In N.E. Ulster the working-class are torn in the mill of
exploiting imperial finance; the middle-class there are
weak against the highly concentrated power of the big
Imperialist industrialists. So the N.E. Parliament is only a
gilded dust-bin around which Belfast derelicts collect for
crusts and partition marks the new Pale.

All those who have passed into the service of the State
machine have betrayed the Irish cause. We must build on
those alone who are being crushed by it, and who alone
have the will and the power to smash it. It will not be dis-
mantled from the top: it cannot be geared to exploit slowly:
a change of drivers is no good, for it is the same machine
with the same nature and the same tasks. On the ruin of
their State we must build ours; we must organise to smash
theirs, rescuing the masses from their illusions about it....

Here, then, is our declaration of allegiance to an Irish
Republic with power in the hands of those alone who can
really achieve freedom, and when achieved, defend it. We
call on all those who share our ideals and believe in our
means to set their hands and their heads to the task before
us.[1]

The new organisation set itself fourteen objectives, most of
which remained part of MacBride's political philosophy. But
a major communistic input was also clearly visible. This latter
element was seized upon to launch an even more ferocious
counterattack by church and state. Since MacBride was the
chairman of Saor Eire, he bore most of the opprobrium. He
was effectively marked out as a bogeyman by the authorities.

MacBride had to read out the Constitution because there were not enough copies to give to the audience in the Iona Hall. He also had to inform the gathering that the hall had been surrounded by the police. The Constitution read in part:

SAOR EIRE
(An Organisation of Workers and Working Farmers)

Objects

1. To break the connection with England....
2. To vest all political power within the Republic....
3. To abolish, without compensation, landlordism in land, fisheries and minerals.
4. To develop the Agricultural Industry, the Fishing Industry, the Mineral resources, by State credits, through Industrial and Workers' Co-operatives.
5. To establish a State monopoly in Banking and Credits.
6. To establish a State monopoly in Export and Import services.
7. To have all forms of Public Inland Transport taken over by the State.
8. To make provision of Housing for citizens a State matter.
9. To guarantee a minimum standard of living for each citizen.
10. To establish a Social Insurance Scheme for old age, widows, orphans, and for the maintenance of the physically and mentally incapacitated.
11. To end the payment of every form of Imperial Tribute.
12. To restore and foster the Gaelic Culture, Language and pastimes.
13. To bring about the closest co-operation between workers in agricultural and in rural districts, and those in towns and cities; to bring them to realise that their interests are mutual; that, therefore, they should be allies, as they are all victims of the same exploiting agencies.[2]

Speaking in the Dáil one week later, William Cosgrave said in condemnation of Saor Eire and the idea that a minority have a right to resort to violence against the state:

Modern States have selected parliamentary institutions as the best method so far devised for giving effect to the majority will of the people. Intimidation, violence and murder are the antithesis of rule by Parliament. The two cannot co-exist and the Government that allows violent methods to grow within the State is itself aiding and abetting the destruction of Parliamentary rule.

Murder, conspiracy and intimidation are being used against the people. It is to put an end to this tyranny that we are setting up a better machinery for the detection and punishment of the criminals.

The doctrine that a group within the Nation can use violence to change the form of Government or merely a part of the Constitution, once accepted, becomes a perpetual menace to the State, no matter what its form. If you excuse violence today because there is an oath of allegiance to the Constitution, you must excuse it tomorrow because property is not socialised, or for some other group theory. No State is accepted in its entirety by all the citizens, and if violence is once tolerated it becomes the normal method for bringing about every change.

We believe that the new patriotism based on Muscovite teachings with a sugar coating of Irish extremism is completely alien to Irish tradition. The right to private property is a fundamental of Christian civilisation and so long as this Government remains in power it will maintain that sacred right for the people. The right to private property was the first citadel attacked by the Russian Communists in their own country, and when it fell the whole fabric of Christianity in Russia fell with it.[3]

The Cosgrove Government had long felt that the new State deserved more support from the Catholic Church than it received. After the murder of Kevin O'Higgins in 1927, Archbishop Byrne of Dublin issued a pastoral letter condemning the deed. But the secretary of the Department of External Affairs, Joseph P. Walsh, wrote a memoranda criticising the fact that Byrne had led people to believe that 'there is no difference between murdering a man set up by the people as one of their rulers and murdering a private citizen'.[4] One way the government had moved to rectify this situation, was to seek to establish diplomatic relations with the Vatican. It felt that if it had a Papal Nuncio in Dublin, he would exercise a certain influence over the local bishops and be a conduit for unbiased information to the Church authorities in Rome. The State too, felt the need to have its own representative at the Vatican. This was particularly required to counteract the negative influence exercised there by the Rector of the Irish College, Monsignor John Hagan. Hagan had advised de Valera to set up Fianna Fáil and seek political power, when he had visited Rome with Seán MacBride in the mid 1920s. MacBride, who was operating as secretary and interpreter to de Valera at the time, totally opposed this move. The Government faced much opposition in their diplomatic quest. The bishops opposed it as did the British government. But eventually in January 1930 the Papal Nuncio arrived to a massive public welcome in Dublin. He was Paschal Robinson, a Dubliner, who had joined the Franciscans and became a very experienced Vatican diplomat. The Government appointed Charles Bewley, an Oxford graduate and a leading member of the Irish Bar, as its first envoy to the Vatican. The Cosgrove government now felt that it could hope for more backing from the bishops. It was so frightened by the Saor Eire conspiracy that it briefed Cardinal MacRory on the matter. It circulated memoranda on the subversion and conspiracy against the State to all the bishops in September 1931, as the hierarchy prepared a major offensive against Saor Eire. There is little doubt that the government was as much afraid of Fianna Fáil taking over, as the IRA, that is if it differentiated at all between the two. De Valera was trying hard not to be demonised with the IRA, as he was received by the Cardinal. But he was not helped when one of his chief lieutenants, Frank Aiken, called in the Dáil for all-party talks with Saor Eire. Two days later, on 18 October 1931, the Catholic bishops issued a joint pastoral. It was a most trenchant statement, denouncing the IRA and the 'Bolshevistic' Saor Eire. Part of it read:

Dearly beloved in Christ,

Assembled in Maynooth for our annual October meeting and deeply conscious of our responsibility for the Faith and

Morals of our people, we cannot remain silent in the face of the growing evidence of a campaign of Revolution and Communism, which if allowed to run its course unchecked must end in the ruin of Ireland, both body and soul.

You have not to be told that there is in active operation amongst us a society of a militarist character whose avowed object is to overthrow the State by force of arms....

Side by side with the society referred to is a new organisation entitled 'Saor Eire' which is frankly communistic in its aims.

This organisation, which is but a translation into Irish life, under Bolshevistic tuition, of a similar scheme in use in Russia....

It is our duty to tell people plainly that the two organisations, whether separate or in alliance, are sinful and irreligious and that no Catholic can lawfully be a member of them.

Once again though, the government was not entirely happy with the bishops' condemnation. Joseph P. Walsh, secretary of the Department of External Affairs, protested to Paschal Robinson that the bishops should have been more condemnatory. He met with Robinson on the matter for over three hours, but with little success. He then instructed Charles Bewley, who was visiting the Department at the time, to see Robinson, and try to alert him to the threat of communism in Ireland. Bewley met Robinson over lunch. But before Bewley could broach the topic he was instructed on, Robinson took the initiative. He said, 'Seán MacBride was here with me yesterday. A nice fellow'. Bewley asked, 'Your Excellency didn't find him a dangerous communist?' 'No, I didn't notice it', Robinson replied disposing of the matter.[5] This episode demonstrates, among other things, that MacBride, though still only twenty seven years old, was no mean diplomatist himself.

Seán MacBride did not savour being denounced by the bishops and the episode embittered him against the left-wingers within the IRA; he felt that when the condemnations were flying, he was left exposed. On the next occasion in 1934 when the radicals were to resort to founding a new movement, he showed them little sympathy.

The majority of the Irish people were totally against the Saor Eire programme. It provoked a major backlash, particularly against MacBride himself. The organisation was declared unlawful, along with the IRA, Cumann na mBan, Maud MacBride's WPDL, and eight other fringe bodies. A military tribunal was reintroduced. Once more, the main open opposition to these measures was provided by Madame MacBride and her women colleagues who merely changed the name of their banned body to People's Rights Association. Although they were expelled from their offices, they continued to protest publicly. Roebuck House was continually raided, and Seán MacBride became public enemy number one of the State security forces.

9

Negotiates with de Valera

William Cosgrave decided to call a general election early in
1932. The IRA and other banned organisations had no problem
deciding on what their attitude should be. 'Put Cosgrave Out'
was their slogan, though they were in no way enamoured of
Fianna Fáil or its platform, which did not even mention the
Republic. The election results were: Fianna Fáil 72, Cumann
na nGaedhal 57, Labour 7, Farmers 3, Others 14. On 9 March
Eamon de Valera was elected president of the executive council by 81 votes, to 68 for Cosgrave. The 'Legion of the Rearguard'
had taken control of the state, holding that the defects of the
Treaty were not their doing. De Valera's mental gymnastics
had taken him to what he regarded as his rightful position, as
the true disciple of 1916. But many of his estranged republican
allies knew that he and his party were not as pure as they
claimed to be. These allies were now full of expectation about
what the new government would do. Many felt that the
Republic was but a blink away.

The outgoing government had placed enormous faith in
their new democratic institutions. Some had feared a coup
d'état from different quarters. The institutions of the State,
the church, and the Establishment, waited with baited breath
to see what would happen as the former IRA men took over.
Great credit is due to both sides that the handover of control
went so smoothly. The civil servants, the police force and the
national army wondered what the future held for them, but
they all behaved well and the new Ministers of State took over
their portfolios with ease.

De Valera knew he had to move quickly to placate the IRA and meet the expectations of his own supporters. The new Minister for Defence, Frank Aiken, went with the Justice Minister James Geoghegan, to the military prison at Arbour Hill to consult with the senior IRA man George Gilmore, imprisoned there. The next day the prisoners were released. A huge rally was held at College Green to welcome their return. Madame MacBride, who had worked so hard on their behalf, was on the platform. She spoke vehemently against the outgoing government, expressing the hope that the imprisoning of republicans, including her son, was now a thing of the past and that her WDPL could be safely disbanded.

The holding of the Eucharistic Congress in June 1932 played a huge part in focusing the minds of the people on something other than politics. The eyes of the Catholic world would be on Ireland, and everybody was determined to show the country in a good light. It also afforded the new government an opportunity to demonstrate to the Catholic Church that Fianna Fáil was a secure guardian of the rights of Catholics.

The IRA initiated talks with de Valera to ascertain how he saw the future. These talks went on for two years. Seán Russell, a straightforward militarist, and George Gilmore, a committed left-winger, conducted the talks at first. De Valera was reasonably clear that the programme for his government was as indicated in the election manifesto: the end of the oath to the British sovereign, an industrial programme, and a cessation of the land annuities to Britain. He felt that there was now no need for the continued existence of the IRA.

Yet the IRA was being inundated with new recruits. Many thought the organisation would be incorporated into the national army. The IRA suddenly became fashionable, as a probable means of advancement within the State. Many IRA men saw things de Valera's way and joined the State apparatus when the opportunity offered. Frank Aiken offered Seán MacBride a commission in the army with the rank of major general. MacBride was insulted by the offer and rejected it immediately.

He was subsequently offered a job as a subeditor with *The Irish Press*. This newspaper had been set up by de Valera in 1931 as a republican paper which would support Fianna Fáil.

It was MacBride's first job. He hated every minute of his time at the newspaper and he was glad to abandon it. He was not cut out to do a nine to five job, either by temperament or ambition. He knew he was meant for greater things.

In the early 1930s the jam factory had been closed down. Seán then asked Louie O'Brien to stay on as his secretary for IRA activities. She did this and was paid a small salary. She attended all the conventions with him and was privy to most of what was going on.

By July 1932 Madame MacBride had decided that de Valera was already reneging on his promises. She believed that the Special Branch of the police was still spying on republicans and imprisoning some of them. She decided to restart her WPDL and her weekly street meetings on behalf of prisoners.

De Valera decided to go to the country early in 1933 to seek a stronger mandate for his programme. Once more the IRA, including Seán MacBride, had to consider their position. They felt that de Valera had made some progress and that since the IRA was now operating openly, it should maintain an anti-Cosgrave line. They began to harass election meetings held by Cosgrave supporters. The latter set up an Army Comrades Association (ACA) to offset the IRA's intimidation. Its leader was T.F.O'Higgins, the brother of the assassinated minister Kevin O'Higgins. Tension and friction developed between the two bodies. De Valera did not intervene and the IRA assumed it was being encouraged to continue. But in a speech at Navan during the election campaign, de Valera said: 'No section of the community will be allowed to arm. All arms shall be completely at the disposal of the majority of the elected representatives of the people.'[1] The IRA believed this comment was aimed at the ACA, which was being pressed to arm like the IRA.

William Cosgrave was not an imaginative politician. He did not offer the electorate any hope of major economic improvement or introduce any new element into the campaign. De Valera was playing to all sections of the community, though he well realised he was under grave suspicion by the Establishment. In the event, he gained five seats and Cosgrave lost nine. The full result was: Fianna Fáil 77, Cumann na nGaedhal 48, Centre Party 11, Labour 8, Others 9. The Centre Party was a revamped Farmers' Party. De Valera had an overall majority of one, but the Labour Party generally supported him over the next four years.

After this victory, de Valera resumed his discussions with the IRA. This time Seán MacBride was the main negotiator. It was a dangerous time because the ACA was developing into a form of National Guard and it was clear that it intended to play a direct part in national affairs. The dismissed Commissioner of Police, Eoin O'Duffy, became its leader. He adopted a Blueshirt military-style uniform for the group. It was, in effect, another private army within the State.

Seán MacBride held several lengthy meetings with de Valera over the next eighteen months to explore their mutual positions. Although the two men knew each other fairly well, de Valera was not an easy person with whom to negotiate. He liked to do most of the talking. For the past fourteen years he had obviously worked out the justification for his actions. He felt almost that he was the embodiment of the State declared by his comrades in 1916, and believed that all true republicans should row in behind him.

But MacBride was no easy target for de Valera's convoluted rhetoric. He had history on his side. His father had been among those executed in 1916 when de Valera had escaped death because of his American citizenship. MacBride had been to London for the Treaty negotiations, though only in a minor capacity, while de Valera decided not to go. MacBride's record of militancy against the Treaty, including his many periods in jail, gave him the moral authority to challenge de Valera on many fundamental points on the authority of the State. This MacBride did, much to de Valera's annoyance.

The lawyer in MacBride enjoyed taking on the disciple of Machiavelli. De Valera insisted that majority rule had to be accepted now. MacBride retorted that de Valera did not accept majority rule in 1916 or in 1926. De Valera said that now the Oath had been removed, it was perfectly correct to enter the Dáil. The achievement of the Republic would only be a matter of time, he said. MacBride countered by saying that majority rule was a perfectly laudable principle for a free people, but that Ireland was not free or united, so the matter did not arise. On top of that, MacBride asserted that de Valera had taken on most of the senior civil servants from the previous regime. These, he claimed, were mostly British secret service agents and should be dismissed. De Valera became indignant, saying that their loyalty was not in any doubt.

MacBride wrote to Joseph MacGarrity, leader of Clan na Gael in the United States about these meetings. In his letter he says of de Valera: 'he is a very hard person to argue with and he spent a tremendous amount of time reiterating his position and justifying his actions in 1921-22-23 and 27. I found it extremely hard to get him to consider anything but his own point of view. His personality is strong and being conscious of this, he plays on it, with the result I found our protracted interviews of little practical value. He always tried to put me in the position of having to be blunt and of even having to hurt his personality, before taking cognisance of our own point of view. He would then put his integrity and judgement against my argument.'

At their last meeting, MacBride again suggested that there should be some informal connection between the IRA and Fianna Fáil, but de Valera would not hear of it. MacBride said that unless there was some accommodation, trouble would inevitably arise. He contended that such inflexibility had probably led to the Civil War. MacBride also reminded de Valera that he then had up to fifty republican prisoners in his jails and that this sort of thing 'could certainly tell his pro-Treaty critics, he was maintaining law and order'. De Valera got very annoyed 'or pretended to lose his temper. He got excited and said he would maintain law and order, even if it cost him his life'.[2]

These discussions led nowhere. Indeed they also cast a cloud of suspicion over MacBride with some of his IRA colleagues, who, knowing MacBride's previous connection with de Valera, feared that he might have been swayed by him.

De Valera set up an Army Volunteer Reserve to give IRA volunteers an opportunity to become legitimate soldiers and have a stake in the state apparatus. He also expanded the army pensions to cover anti-Treaty veterans. Once again, the IRA was heavily depleted as men faced up to the fact of the Free State.

In 1934 de Valera had written to Joseph McGarrity, claiming that he had no alternative but to curb the IRA: 'We have undertaken a responsibility to the people at present living, to the future and to the dead. We will not allow any group of individuals to prevent us carrying it out.'[3]

10

IRA Tactician and Chief of Staff

After their unimpeded harassment by the IRA during the 1932 and the 1933 general elections, the Cumann na nGael party decided they required some group to counter their adversaries. They needed to protect their legitimate interests in the State they had created, against the left-wing IRA and the new government itself, if necessary. They decided to re-organise their own Army Comrades Association, which had been formed to look after the welfare of ex-soldiers from the National Army. This group then became an active political, if not military, force. When in 1933 de Valera decided to sack the long-time Commissioner of Police, General O'Duffy, because he lacked confidence in him, O'Duffy was appointed head of the renewed Army Comrades Association. This body which changed its name to the National Guard, adopted a blue shirt as a uniform for its members, giving it a decidedly military look. It was then commonly referred to as The Blueshirts, and it was often compared to European fascist groups. De Valera reacted quickly to this development and withdrew all licences to carry firearms in an effort to stymy its potential military threat. The Blueshirts and the IRA clashed around the country while everybody waited to see how de Valera handled the situation.

The Blueshirts presented the depleted IRA with just the motivation it required to regroup and recharge its fundamental idea: that the future wellbeing of the country required a vigorous republican army. O'Duffy's National Guard blossomed around the country. It decided that it could be just as militant as the IRA in protecting its own interests and the State. The

IRA responded to the challenge and prepared for open confrontation. The government forces kept a low profile, but de Valera was waiting to pounce. Echoing events in Italy, O'Duffy decided this his 'army' would march on Dublin en route to a ceremony in Glasnevin cemetery to honour the founders of the State, Collins, Griffith and O'Higgins on 13 August 1933. The smell of a coup d'état was in the air. The IRA mobilised a huge army in Dublin to attack the Blueshirts. They doubted the loyalty of the State security forces to suppress a coup.

In July de Valera had recalled all legally held arms, most of which belonged to those who had supported the Treaty. The new Commissioner of Police, Colonel Eamon Broy, hastily recruited large numbers of ex-IRA men into an armed section of the police force and positioned them at all government installations. During the early hours of 13 August, de Valera declared the march illegal. He also banned the National Guard, using the notorious Section 2A of the Free State Constitution. The march was cancelled.

In the following month various pro-Treaty groups came together to form a new United Ireland Party, called Fine Gael. It elected Eoin O'Duffy as leader, though Cosgrave was the party's parliamentary leader. The IRA regarded this as a dangerous development, and clashes between its members and the Blueshirts continued throughout the country. This inevitably led to IRA men being arrested and facing the military tribunal.

More and more, republicans were coming to feel that de Valera was right and that Fianna Fáil was the way forward. The sensible course for any man interested in a future for himself and his family was to accept the status quo — as a staging post. Many of those within the IRA felt that some political movement was necessary if Fianna Fáil was to be challenged in a radical way. The Army Council was again riven between the different groups. MacBride felt that there was little possibility of a 'new departure' having popular success against Fianna Fáil. As Seán Cronin says, MacBride was the 'chief political tactician of the I.R.A. in the thirties'.[1] The IRA was badly split on the issue. The left wingers decided to go ahead without the sanction of the Army Council, and set up a new Republican Congress. They issued a manifesto from their first conference in Athlone in April 1934: 'We believe that a Republic of a United Ireland will never be achieved except through a struggle which uproots capitalism on its way. We cannot conceive of a free Ireland with a subject working class: we cannot conceive of a subject Ireland with a free working class.'

The IRA expelled the Congress leaders from its ranks. The Congress itself split shortly afterwards and eventually passed into oblivion. But it served to damage the IRA. The Bishop of Waterford, Dr Kinnane, sacked a teacher, Frank Edwards, for attending the Congress. The bishop did not distinguish between the Congress and the IRA, much to MacBride's annoyance, and condemned the IRA as 'the most anti-patriotic and anti-religious group that was ever attempted to be foisted on this country'. Dr Kinnane also saw that all the other Catholic bishops joined his condemnation, declaring that even to attend an IRA meeting was gravely sinful.

Gradually the IRA, despite MacBride's best attempts, came more and more into open conflict with de Valera's security forces. They got involved in trades disputes and local intimidation. MacBride, fearing that open conflict was inevitable, proposed within the Army Council that a republican political party, which would not be left wing, was essential. His proposal was defeated, amid a certain grave suspicion of his change of tactics.

The militants were looking for action. They found it in a transport strike by bus workers in Dublin in 1935. The government had brought in the army to break the strike. The IRA attacked the army and the police. De Valera reacted immediately and arrested up to fifty leading IRA men saying 'there was only one thing the Government could do'.[2] The military tribunal gave heavy sentences to some, including Tom Barry, who did not recognise the court and refused to answer questions. Soon over 100 republicans were in prison and more were to follow. In June 1935 over 10,000 people attended a ceremony at Wolfe Tone's grave at Bodenstown, County Kildare to hear MacBride give a defiant oration on behalf of the IRA. The enmity between the IRA and Fianna Fáil grew to hatred. Once more IRA members were harassed and followed by the police. The Army Council was under pressure to hit back at Fianna Fáil, but the only way they could do so was, as MacBride advised, by political means. Eventually, at MacBride's instigation, they approved an abstentionist political party, Cumann Poblachta na hEireann, in 1936. The rank and file members of the IRA were very suspicious of the new party, since all members who had previously sought to take the political path had ended up outside a weakened IRA. Their wish was for military action against the Free State or against the British in Northern Ireland or indeed in Britain itself.

Cumann Poblachta na hEireann was designed to be an alternative to the earlier abortive and divisive Republican Congress, without its extreme policies. The party fought the local elections in June, but none of its candidates was elected. Madame MacBride, at the age of sixty-nine, stood as a candidate. She also sat on the party's national executive, but it had no future, being just another splinter abstentionist, Sinn Féin type of grouping. It held its one and only Ard Fheis in November 1936 at Wynn's Hotel in Dublin.

The IRA had committed some vicious murders in the Free State, which de Valera could not ignore. History repeated itself when in June 1936 the Minister for Justice, Gerald Boland, declared the IRA an 'unlawful association'. He invoked Section 2A of the Free State Constitution and banned the annual IRA public meeting and procession at Bodenstown. MacBride had to abandon his wife and two children at Roebuck House and go on the run once more. His mother took to the streets in protest, organising regular meetings in O'Connell Street, Dublin. One of her speakers, Patrick McKenna, was arrested and sentenced to eighteen months in jail by a military tribunal for his participation.[3]

The chief of staff of the IRA, Seamus Twomey, was also arrested and sentenced to three years imprisonment on 19 June. His assistant, Jim Killeen, had earlier been sentenced in Northern Ireland to a seven-year jail term. This threw the GHQ into a turmoil. The Army Council met and nominated Seán MacBride to be the new chief of staff, pending a general army convention, which constitutionally was the body to make such appointments. This appointment of MacBride was a logical move, since he was a senior figure who had had experience of every aspect of the work of the organisation. He had an intelligent and meticulous legal mind and could be relied upon to be careful not to take any sudden policy decisions, without due preparation and consultation.

But MacBride spoke with a French accent and he was very different from the average volunteer or officer. Many IRA members also regarded him as too intelligent by half. The anti-intellectual, peasant, rather begrudging Irish attitude came into play whenever MacBride's name was put forward. His meetings with de Valera and his Cumann na Poblachta were also held against him. All this antipathy to MacBride became focussed in the person of Seán Russell, a straightforward though simple militarist. Russell felt that the IRA was an army pure and simple, and he had no time for those advocating left- or right-wing politics. He was in charge of procuring and storing arms and ammunitions for the IRA and believed that his people should be using them against their enemies and not engaging in so much talk.

Russell ignored MacBride's new position and continued to do what he had been at for years. But, like most new commanders, MacBride had his own ideas. He wanted to know precisely what was happening within GHQ and instituted new procedures of accountability for materials and funds. Russell ignored the new procedures, and the meticulous MacBride soon built up a dossier of charges against him. Under a court martial, Russell could not account for certain monies that had been under his control. He was found guilty and was expelled from the organisation. This was to prove a Pyrrhic victory. Many believed that Russell was an honest man and that his idea of mounting a subversive campaign in England was a good one. Still, life proceeded smoothly under MacBride's careful leadership, though the feeling that, despite everything, he really was not one of them, grew.

Meanwhile, Russell toured the country, meeting IRA volunteers. He told them that he had been hard done by and that as long as MacBride led the movement, it would never 'take the field'. Russell canvassed the volunteers to vote against MacBride at the next convention.

MacBride wrote to Joseph McGarrity in June 1936, saying:

Beyond the fact that the situation is rather uncomfortable for those of us who are on the run or in jail, the position on the whole is good. The Free State Government have clarified the position and have now taken exactly the same stand as their predecessors. While nationally this is regrettable, it clears the decks as far as we are concerned. We have steadily tried to avoid pushing de Valera into the position occupied by Cosgrave, but apparently he was bent on occupying that position himself.[4]

Very few republicans, if any, would admit to being 'intellectual'; for them, the word would have negative connotations. Anyone given to such tendencies would be mocked and regarded perversely as looking down on his colleagues. Seán MacBride was an intellectual. He took little interest in the mundane matters of many of his colleagues.

The noted Irish writer, Mairtín Ó Cadhain, told the story of the IRA holding a weekend Army Council meeting in August 1936 in Dublin, with MacBride in the chair. On the Sunday morning, MacBride noticed that a certain restlessness had arisen among the group. He asked Ó Cadhain what the matter was. Ó Cadhain informed him that Mayo and Kerry were playing in the All Ireland football semi-final that afternoon in Roscommon and many of the group wanted to attend. According to Ó Cadhain, MacBride's reaction was: 'So a game of football is more important than the future of the Irish Republic'.[5] Such a remark displayed a frightening lack of appreciation of the culture of Gaelic sport in Ireland.

Abstentionist republican candidates George Plunkett and Stephen Hayes, stood in by-elections in Galway and Wexford during August 1936, but were whitewashed by Fianna Fáil. This was a blow to MacBride's ambitions for Cumann na Poblachta and gravely weakened his position.

The Spanish Civil War was in progress. A former IRA man, Frank Ryan, was seeking to organise the remnants of the Republican Congress and any IRA people he could convince, to travel to Spain to fight for the Republic. Many volunteers joined him.

Against this background an army convention was held. It was again split by various factions. Tom Barry of Cork urged

IRA attacks on the British within Northern Ireland. This view carried the day at the convention, though senior members including MacBride opposed it. The Army Council decided against ratifying MacBride as chief of staff and installed Barry instead. It was a bitter pill for MacBride, after a lifetime of dedication to the IRA. But to quote J. Bowyer-Bell: 'Despite his 1916 name the average Volunteer felt MacBride was a strange Irishman: he had a peculiar accent, too much education, and was very, very clever. More than his politics within the Army or his plans for the future, it was his "differentness" which apparently grated, making him unpopular for a variety of often contradictory reasons.'[6] MacBride was not a wily enough politician to manipulate the various factions and he left himself exposed to dismissal. His enemies were jubilant, especially Seán Russell and his militant supporters. The Army Council felt that the policy of attacking the British within Northern Ireland was a foolhardy one though it was what the volunteers wanted. Since it was Barry's idea, they decided to give him control of the army. Barry was a folk hero to the volunteers around the country, while MacBride attracted indifference and even hostility. Tom Barry appointed MacBride as his intelligence officer at GHQ. Preparations for action within the North commenced. Members of the IRA in the Six Counties who had little representation at Army Council level, were thrilled that, at last, they were being considered.

MacBride took no further active part in the IRA. His removal from the leadership was the worst thing that could have happened to him. It would have broken a lesser spirit but, not given to tardiness, he was able to persuade University College to accept his earlier period of law studies and he was able to continue with that. Although other members of the IRA headquarters staff were paid a small wage, he had never taken a penny.

Meantime Seán Russell had been in the USA since April, defending himself against the verdict of the court martial. He succeeded in convincing Clann na Gael that a military campaign in England was a good idea. They offered to finance it, if Russell could rehabilitate himself within the IRA.

The GHQ had completed the planning and logistical work for the war in the North, which was to commence with an attack on Armagh Military Barracks. Tom Barry had relied heavily on his own Cork brigade for the operation. At the last minute, GHQ discovered that its 'top secret operation' was common knowledge in all republican circles. The British, they were sure, were just waiting for them to arrive. Barry was humiliated by the debacle and decided to resign as chief of staff and return to Cork.

The Army Council could have restored MacBride to his former position, but he was passed over. He was simply regarded as another failed politician. Seán Russell's supporters tried to get somebody elected who would be favourably disposed to a campaign in England. In the event, a compromise candidate, Michael Fitzpatrick, was appointed, who brought new and younger men into GHQ. MacBride was out in the cold. But worse was to happen the next year when the general army convention met in April 1938. Seán Russell returned triumphant and was elected chief of staff, with a mandate to start a bombing campaign in England. This proved too much for many stalwarts and, after a divisive convention, much of the old guard resigned.

The precise timing of MacBride's departure from the IRA remains open to speculation. Seán Cronin says in a footnote in his *Irish Nationalism* (page 281) that MacBride left the movement in June 1938, after Russell's plans had been endorsed. Margaret Ward in *Maud Gonne* (p. 175) accepts the same general timing, as does Bowyer-Bell in *The IRA*. Michael Farrell, writing in *Magill* (at Christmas 1982) says the same. But in the next issue he has a correction, presumably from MacBride himself, to say that he left the IRA in 1937. MacBride said that de Valera's 1937 Constitution marked his turning point away from the IRA. But his rejection cut deeply. In any case the IRA was probably not the kind of organisation to which one sent one's formal resignation.

MacBride did not break all connections with the IRA in that he subsequently defended members in the courts free of charge. Louie O'Brien also ceased to have anything more to do with the IRA at this time. She got married in 1936 and received a print of Roger Casement from MacBride as a wedding present; it was a limited edition print of Casement in the dock in London in 1916, a work by Fanto of Saxony. Louie

O'Brien continued to carry out MacBride's secretarial work, but now in connection with his legal studies. It was an unpaid position.

11

Earning a Living

Eamon de Valera called a general election for July 1937. He also decided to put forward a new Constitution for ratification by the electorate on the same day. This Constitution was opposed by republicans, since there was no mention of a Republic and it seemed to accept the fact of partition. Maud MacBride earlier had begun to put out a small news-sheet called *Prison Bars* because so many republican journals had been banned. She highlighted one of the controversies provoked by the Constitution — the position of women. The July 1937 number of *Prison Bars* was devoted to the issue. *The Irish Press* also gave much coverage to this aspect of the controversy. *Prison Bars* said of the Constitution: 'Mr de Valera shows the mawkish distrust of women which has always coloured his outlook. We have the Proclamation of the Republic as a noble clear concise Document, as our Charter of Liberty ... the Article concerning women and the Articles providing for Special Courts would damn it in my eyes.'

The Constitution recognised 'the special position of the Holy Catholic Apostolic and Roman Church as the guardian of the Faith professed by the great majority of its citizens' (Article 44.2). Articles 2 and 3 spoke about the nation and were the two fundamental political statements that de Valera hoped would satisfy all shades of opinion. Article 2 read: 'The National Territory consists of the whole island of Ireland, its islands and the territorial seas'. Article 3 stated: 'Pending the reintegration of the National territory, and without prejudice to the right of Parliament and Government, established by this constitution to exercise jurisdiction over the whole of that territory, the laws enacted by that Parliament shall have the like area and extent of application, as the laws of Saorstat Eireann and the like extra-territorial effect.' De Valera was claiming *de jure* control of the whole country, but accepted that *de facto*, the Constitution would cover the 26 Counties.[1]

Ireland's economic situation was poor. The economic war over land annuities with Britain had depressed Irish trade. But the government had made progress on the political front. They had abolished the oath of loyalty to the British monarch. They had contained the Blueshirt threat. They had reduced the power of the Crown representative and, following the abdication of Edward VIII, they had removed references to the Crown and Governor General from the old constitution. Fianna Fáil fought the 1937 election on the republican ticket, which included a lavish commemoration at Wolfe Tone's grave. They also claimed to have set aside the IRA.

Despite all this, they lost major support in the general election, dropping 100,000 votes. They lost their overall majority in the Dáil. The detailed results were: Fianna Fáil 69, Fine Gael 48, Labour 13, Others 8. But Fianna Fáil remained in government, relying on Labour Party support. The new Constitution was carried by 685,105 to 526,945 votes: not a huge margin, but sufficient.

De Valera was shaken by the election result and resolved to seek to improve the economy. He no longer thought it necessary to leave the British Commonwealth to establish freedom. He had entered into a coal and cattle pact with the British government.[2] Now he decided to try to end the economic war entirely. In this he was successful. For a cash payment of £10 million, the United Kingdom cancelled a claim for £100 million. Restrictions of Irish agricultural exports to the UK were lifted and preferential treatment was given to British industrial imports. But very importantly for his claim to be a true republican, de Valera got the British to leave the Irish ports they had controlled under the Treaty. The success of his Anglo-Irish Agreement was remarkable and he decided to call a snap general election in June 1938, less than one year after the previous one. This time he was triumphant. The results were: Fianna Fáil 77, Fine Gael 45, Labour 9, Others 7. Fianna Fáil had emerged from its sectional power base to become a mainstream party. Partition was now the only continuing political problem on the nationalist agenda, although some people still longed for a declaration of a 'Republic'.

The general economic malaise that affected the country had its repercussions in Roebuck House. Seán's wife, Kid, took a job with the Irish Sweepstakes. The Irish Hospitals Sweepstake was a lottery company set up, among others, by an old IRA man named Joseph McGrath. Although he had voted for the Treaty, jobs were given to all shades of republicans. Much of the money spent on buying tickets for the draws on various horse races came from the United Kingdom and the United States. The legality of such ticket selling, particularly in the USA was challenged. This led to various subterfuges. One of these was to establish private agents in Ireland to whom the stubs of sold tickets and the collected cash could be posted. These agents then paid the Sweeps for the tickets in Irish currency. There was a large margin available in the currency exchange, which the agents were allowed to keep for their services. Kid MacBride and Louie O'Brien handled ticket sales for a few years until a change in regulation in the United States rendered their agencies obsolete. But for some years they earned considerable sums of money.

Maud decided to write an autobiography up to the point of her marriage to Major John MacBride. She also decided to be very circumspect with some details of her past life which might reflect badly on Seán.

The MacBride household had always enjoyed a high standard of living. They were part of the upper class, though on the extreme republican wing. Maud was one of the most famous ladies in Ireland and was much revered for her steadfastness. She greatly enjoyed Seán and Kid's extended family and their two children, Anna and Tiernan (B 1934). She liked having people around her. She had bought a cottage in Laragh, County Wicklow for Iseult and Francis Stuart and their two children. There was nothing she liked more than having them all together at Roebuck.

Louie O'Brien regarded Maud as bordering on sainthood. The only person she can remember Maud being critical of was Francis Stuart. Iseult would come back to Roebuck telling awful stories about him, and Maud would take her side.

During the 1930s Maud and Seán decided to convert the Gonne legacy into Irish Government Bonds from its American base. This was a courageous move, but it also meant a significant drop in their family income.

Kid took over the management of Roebuck. It says a lot for her spirit and character that she was able to coexist so perfectly with Maud, particularly with her husband absent for so much of the time. Although Maud was getting old, she continued to take a stand on every issue where prisoners' rights and republicanism was involved. To a large extent she became dedicated to her son's career and future.

Despite these changes, Roebuck remained a very well-to-do establishment, as Louie O'Brien recalls during the early years of the war and the Emergency.

When World War II began, Louie had gone to live on the northside of the city with her husband and their child. The buses would cease operation at 9 pm and she began to feel cut off and isolated because all her friends were on the southside. Her husband was a commercial traveller and was away during the week. Seán MacBride suggested that the O'Briens should move in to the top storey of Roebuck House. They did this, supposedly for the duration of the war years, but it came to be an almost permanent arrangement. At that time the servants at Roebuck included a chauffeur, cook, parlour maid, kitchen maid, sewing maid and two gardeners. Louie O'Brien also employed a maid.

12

Counsel for Prisoners

In January 1939 word reached Roebuck House that W.B. Yeats had died on the French Riviera. He had been in failing health for some time. During the 1930s after he had resigned from the Free State Senate, Yeats had become reconciled with his old love, Maud. His death was a deep loss to her and her family. Iseult and Seán, in a certain sense, had been his children. He had known them intimately all their lives and had looked after their interests on many occasions. Although he was a Nobel laureate and the most famous poet of his age, most of all he was a friend to the MacBride family. He loved their mother; loved the children. Luckily, all the bitterness that had developed had mellowed.

The following month the IRA published a letter to the British government in the name of 'The Government and Army Council of the Irish Republican Army', demanding that the British evacuate Ireland and 'Issue your Declaration of Abdication in respect of our country'. The letter emphasised that the IRA wanted good relations with Britain and assured the government that Ireland would not act against its interests in the coming conflict. It went on: 'we shall regret if this fundamental feeling is ignored and we are compelled to intervene actively in the military and commercial life of your country as your Government is now intervening in ours'.[1]

Seán Russell was determined to attack Britain in her hour of difficulty. A bombing campaign began in Britain, causing consternation, and repressive measures against Irish residents there. Russell talked a 1916 veteran and former colleague of de Valera, Patrick McGrath, into becoming actively involved in the campaign in Ireland. Fianna Fáil set up military tribunals and began to arrest known IRA men. De Valera knew that it was essential for Irish interests that the country did not become embroiled in the European war. To ensure that the British were kept reasonably content with Ireland's neutrality, he had to contain the IRA. Among those arrested on 9 September 1939 was Patrick McGrath. He and others went on hunger strike. A vociferous campaign was initiated to gain his release, but de Valera and his Minister for Justice, Gerald Boland, stood firm. De Valera declared: 'If we let these men out, we are going immediately afterwards to have every single man we have tried to detain and restrain, going on hunger strike.'

Although Seán MacBride had now turned his back on the IRA and violence, he still felt obliged to defend his ex-colleagues against the authorities. For him, the 1937 Constitution was a sufficient incentive to lay down arms and pursue the political path. Nevertheless, he fought assiduously over future years to gain justice for those still engaged in violence. He had inherited his mother's detestation of imprisonment, and he dedicated himself to defending the prisoners and their rights against an increasingly oppressive regime. As the war progressed and Ireland's neutral status became more difficult to defend, the Fianna Fáil government acted vigorously to the continuing IRA campaign. Seán MacBride became the leading legal defender of the IRA.

MacBride appealed the case of the hunger strikers to the High Court, arguing that the Offences Against the State Act, under which the men had been interned was unconstitutional. He was using de Valera's own constitution as a weapon against him. Judge Gavan Duffy (who was a signatory to the Treaty), agreed with MacBride's submission and the fifty three internees were released on 1 December 1939.

The same month, December 1939, the IRA launched an audacious raid on the army Magazine Fort in Dublin's Phoenix Park. The government introduced an Emergency Powers Bill closing the legal loophole that MacBride had uncovered in the courts, but the IRA's campaign continued.

Internment resumed once more. Again the prisoners went on hunger strikes demanding political status. This was a claim made by de Valera himself in the past, when he had been jailed. But his Minister for Justice, Gerald Boland, also a former IRA man, was utterly determined to show no weakness towards the hunger strikers. In April 1940 two of them, Tony D'Arcy from Galway and Jack MacNeela from Mayo died. At the inquest Boland insisted on appearing himself as a witness for the State. MacBride, who was appearing for the dead men's families, cross-examined him. Boland described this experience as the most frightening ordeal of his life. IRA supporters in court vented their anger at Boland as MacBride asked him, 'Do you realise that the whole country was against the goverment for letting these men die?' Boland held firm, asserting that the people supported the government's stand against the IRA. He said that a forthcoming by-election in Galway, where D'Arcy came from, would give the electorate an opportunity to pass judgement. In the event, Fine Gael refused to run a candidate, and Fianna Fáil won.

In the summer of 1940 two detectives were murdered in Dublin. Among those arrested for the crimes was Patrick McGrath. He was tried before a military court. MacBride defended him, but he was found guilty and was executed in August 1940.

Six teenage IRA volunteers were found guilty of murdering a policeman in Belfast. All were sentenced to death. MacBride organised a reprieve committee in Dublin, which collected 200,000 signatures in a petition. Pressure was put on the USA and the Secretary of State, Cordell Hull, consulted the British Ambassador. Five of the six youths had their sentences commuted, but one, Tommy Williams, was hanged, despite the fact that the Irish government intervened on his behalf.[2]

Eamonn de Valera was a stickler for protocol and due process. His experience in the League of Nations had taught him a lot about the realpolitik of international relations. Defending his neutrality policy in the Dáil, he said: 'I stated in a very definite way that it was the aim of Government policy, in case of a European war, to keep this country, if at all possible, out of it. We have pursued that policy, and I intend to pursue it.'[3] For the duration of World War II, the German Embassy remained open in Dublin. Irish sentiment was strongly pro-German for a long time, on the principle that they were fighting the English.

This was particularly true at Roebuck House. Francis Stuart, Iseult's husband, had got a job lecturing on modern literature at Berlin University. He remained on there, later to part from Iseult and their children.

At that same time a German spy named Hermann Goertz, was preparing to parachute into Ireland. His mission was to seek to incite the IRA to activity in Northern Ireland. Goertz made his way to Stuart's cottage in Laragh on 9 May 1940, where he asked to be put into contact with the IRA. Iseult Stuart complied with this request. But on 22 May the house in Dublin where Goertz was staying was raided by the police. The spy escaped, leaving over $25,000 behind him. A suit in the house was traced to one Iseult had recently purchased in Switzer's of Dublin. This led to her arrest and trial at the Special Criminal Court. She was acquitted of assisting a foreign agent and on 1 July was released. Goertz remained at large for one year, before he was arrested and interned. This episode was very embarrassing at inter-governmental level as both Ireland and Germany were ostensibly on friendly terms. It was also embarrassing for the MacBride family, as the German ambassador was a guest at Roebuck House several times prior to this incident.

The IRA sent a delegation in 1940 to Berlin to negotiate with the Germans on aid for Ireland. On the delegation was MacBride's old enemy, Seán Russell. The Germans were not interested in the internal politics of the IRA or in its hatred of the de Valera government. They wanted the IRA to take direct action in Northern Ireland, which would suit Germany's war needs. Negotiations with the IRA proved difficult and inconclusive. Returning home, Russell was given a radio set and a special code for contact with Germany. The journey was by submarine. Russell became seriously ill on board and died on 14 August 1940, off the coast of Galway. He was buried at sea with full naval honours. Later suspicions arose as to the true cause of his death. In 1950, Seán MacBride, then Minister for External Affairs, was asked in the Dáil if he was in a position to give any information on the circumstances under which Russell had died. He replied: 'It appears reasonably certain that Seán Russell died as a result of illness while a passenger on a German submarine in 1940.'[4]

Ireland became isolated from the rest of the world during the Emergency. The economy faltered badly. Efforts at industrialisation reduced the nation's self-sufficiency. The supply situation was critical and a new shipping company, 'Irish Shipping', was established in 1941 by Seán Lemass, the Minister for supplies. Rationing and the pegging of prices and wages were instituted, and compulsory tillage was introduced on the land. Many Irish people had to emigrate to England to find work. Ireland's defence budget went almost completely on defending the State against the IRA. Censorship kept news of major events away from the people.

MacBride was involved in a host of relentless legal battles with the government over the next few years on behalf of his former colleagues, who believed that if hunger and thirst strikes were right in 1922 and 1923, they were right in the 1940s. During the Emergency, six IRA men were executed, three died on hunger strike, 600 were interned without trial, and another 500 were charged and jailed.

As the war progressed, MacBride regarded Ireland's policy of neutrality as sacrosanct. It united the country behind de Valera although W.T. Cosgrave did suggest that neutrality be abandoned in the event of an imminent invasion. As pressure from Britain and the US mounted, a demand was made that Ireland close down the German and Japanese diplomatic missions in Dublin, MacBride wrote to de Valera on 23 March 1944 in terms many would find strange: 'Dear Chief, If, in the course of the present crisis, my services can be of any value to the Government, I shall be at your disposal. If I may be permitted, I should like also to express my admiration at the manner in which you have handled the situation'.[5] De Valera did not reply to this; by this time he was hostile towards MacBride, whose defence of IRA members during the Emergency had been a thorn in de Valera's side. The fact that MacBride's brother-in-law, Francis Stuart, had decided to stay on in Nazi Germany and become part of the German propaganda machine, was embarrassing for MacBride. Stuart was one of a group of Irishmen who made broadcasts to Ireland in English and Irish for most of the war, suggesting that, in a new order, partition would end.

Francis Stuart's name headed the list, compiled by the Irish Department of External Affairs, of people suspected of supporting the Nazis and of being involved in 'surreptitious' activities in Ireland. Letters to Iseult from Stuart, and her replies, were intercepted by the authorities. He was suspected of paying a secret visit to Ireland during the war.

Although de Valera outwardly maintained a strict protocol with the Axis powers, in secret there was no doubt where Ireland's sympathies lay. A secret memorandum from the Department of External Affairs in May 1941 details the manner in which Ireland was helping the British: providing information on transport and military facilities in Ireland; providing free air space for British planes and broadcasting facilities; the passing on of information collected; a coast watch service; routing of official German and Italian communications through Britain; internment of spies; use of Shannon Airport; blacking out areas at the request of the British.

Another 1941 secret document, released in January 1991, provided for the contingency that if and when Irish forces could no longer resist a German invasion, the chief of staff of the Army would advise the Taoiseach, who would then decide to invite the British in. He would do so in person by speaking to Sir John Maffey, the British representative in Dublin. But the document emphasises that British military must not cross the border until met by liaison officers from the Irish army.[6] The IRA would not have been very happy about such plans, nor would Seán MacBride.

A general election was held in June 1943 and de Valera held on to power, though he lost votes and an overall majority. The results were: Fianna Fáil 67, Fine Gael 32, Labour 17, Clann na Talmhan 10, Farmers 5, Others 7. Clann na Talmhan had been founded in 1938 and derived most of its support from small farmers. Fine Gael had performed disastrously in what should have been favourable circumstances for them. W.T. Cosgrave resigned and was replaced in 1944 as party leader by Richard Mulcahy, who had actually lost his Dáil seat in the 1943 election. A major personality split in the Labour Party between Jim Larkin and William O'Brien tempted de Valera to call a snap election in May 1944.

Fianna Fáil regained an overall majority of seats. The

results were Fianna Fáil 76, Fine Gael 30, Clann na Talmhan 11, Labour 8, National Labour 4, Farmers 2, Others 7. During this time de Valera remained under severe pressure from the British and the Americans to join the Allies in their fight against the Nazis but, with the vast support of the Irish people behind him, he kept Ireland out of the war.

During MacBride's ever-increasing work at the bar, he came into contact with a wide body of political opinion. One of the people to influence him most was a colleague, John A. Costello. 'Costello over a period of years, had persuaded MacBride to exchange his extreme fringe republicanism for constitutional and parliamentary activity.'[7]

When Hitler's death was announced in 1945, de Valera outraged the Allies by calling on the German embassy in Dublin to express his government's formal condolences.

In a victory broadcast the next week, Winston Churchill attacked de Valera's neutrality: 'So much at variance with the temper and instinct of thousands of Southern Irishmen who hastened to the battlefront.... This was indeed a deadly moment in our life, and if it had not been for the loyalty and friendship of Northern Ireland, we should have been forced to come to close quarters with Mr. de Valera.... We left the de Valera Government to frolic with the German and later with the Japanese representatives to their hearts content.'[8]

The end of the war and of military censorship brought revelations to the Irish people of the horrors that had been going on in the contest between the jailed IRA and an unyielding government. In 1946 republican prisoners were still being held naked, in solitary confinement, deprived of all rights. MacBride had fought unsuccessfully throughout the war years to see that they were treated humanely. Committees working for the release of the prisoners were set up throughout the country. For the public, the issue crystalised in the case of one man, Seán McCaughey, a Northerner who went on hunger strike to force the authorities to grant political status. Seán MacBride had become a Senior Counsel in 1943 and was appointed McCaughey's legal representative. On 10 May 1946 Madame MacBride wrote to *The Irish Times*:

Sir,

Those unable to serve can *demand* nothing; therefore I,
who am almost 80 and bedridden, make my last *request*....
I make it to the people and to the Government: Let no more
young lives be sacrificed to uphold an old British rule of
Victorian origin; be speedier than death in releasing young
McCaughey; please, with him, release the others from
Portlaoghise Jail who have been fighting that old British
rule with the same spirit of courage and endurance which
liberated twenty-six of our counties and among whom is the
son of our comrade Lord Mayor McCurtain, who, dying for
Ireland, entrusted his own children to her care. Only when
this is done can our Government and people unitedly,
without hypocrisy, demand that the ill treatment of prisoners in our six occupied counties shall cease.

The Department of Justice refused to concede political status
to the republican prisoners, treating them as ordinary
criminals. The day after Madame MacBride's letter appeared,
McCaughey died. He had been in jail since 1941 and was on
hunger strike for 31 days, the last 12 of which he was also on
thirst strike. At his inquest, Seán MacBride highlighted for
the first time the appalling conditions and treatment inflicted
on the republican prisoners. He drew the desired response
from the doctor when he asked, 'You would not keep a dog in
conditions like that, would you doctor?' MacBride's Junior
Counsel, Noel Hartnett, a member of Fianna Fáil and an
employee of Radio Eireann, lost his job shortly afterwards and
left Fianna Fáil, gradually becoming disillusioned by the
party's retreat from traditional republicanism. Hartnett used
to fill in for another broadcaster on a programme called 'Question Time' during the summer season. He was abruptly
removed from his post despite a protest from Radio Eireann.
He was replaced at short notice by Eamon Andrews, who later
achieved eminence in his field but was then endeavouring to
achieve a breakthrough in Radio.

For a short period at this time MacBride thought of joining
the Labour Party. Louie O'Brien says that she, among others,
talked him out of it, arguing that a new republican party was
called for. Noel Hartnett was now a free political agent with

considerable political know-how. He and MacBride began to collaborate on political affairs. When the lodge at Roebuck House became vacant, Hartnett moved in.

Noel Hartnett was a Kerryman who won a county council scholarship to Trinity College. He followed the family tradition into Fianna Fáil, where he became a member of the national executive, and was a close friend of de Valera. He was devastated when the latter insisted he had to be dismissed from his job with Radio Eireann, because of his legal association with MacBride.

13

Clann na Poblachta

Seán MacBride had not allowed the disappointment of Cumann Poblachta na hEireann dissuade him from a future political effort. In 1946, on St Patrick's Day, at a meeting in the Mansion House in Dublin, he chaired a 'standing committee', elected to consider methods of achieving a thirty-two-county Republic. The committees organised for the release of prisoners after the war were eager to tackle de Valera on a political front. After much planning and discussion, a new party, Clann na Poblachta, was formed in Dublin on 6 July 1946. Its leader was Seán MacBride. From the start the party set out to be as broadly based as possible, concerning itself with social and economic problems. It highlighted 'the low standard of political morality in public life'. MacBride's legal colleague from the McCaughey inquest, Noel Hartnett, was on the executive of the new party. Others on the executive were Michael Fitzpatrick, like MacBride an ex-IRA chief of staff, and Donal O'Donoghue and Jim Killeen, two former IRA adjutants general. The IRA did not look kindly on this new political venture and threatened to expel any of its members who joined the new party.

In a speech to a public meeting in the Mansion House on 5 February 1947, MacBride said:

If there is any reality to any attempt to end partition, we must throw open the door to elected representatives of Northern Ireland. In the Constitution it is claimed that the Dáil is the parliament of the whole country. Yet Mr. de Valera's government refused to allow elected representatives of Northern Ireland to sit in Leinster House. We must face realities and we must realise that if we get a Republic in name, it would mean nothing unless it ensured economic and social freedom for all the people of the country. We have to ensure that no section of the people will be exploited by another section.[1]

This kind of rhetoric proved popular. In June 1947 local elections were held. Fianna Fáil lost ground to Clann na Poblachta. In late October three Dáil by-elections were held together. Clann na Poblachta won two of them on transfer votes from other parties, one in Tipperary, the other in Dublin South-Central, where MacBride was the victorious candidate. He defeated W.T. Mullins, the general secretary of Fianna Fáil.

The period leading up to and subsequent to the by-elections, was a very difficult one for the government. A lengthy transport strike was in progress, with the army providing a skeleton service. A bank strike occurred which obliged the Minister for Finance, Frank Aiken, to order all banks to close to prevent chaos. The country was in the grip of an austere supplementary budget and a pegging of wages. On 13 October, Seán Lemass revealed that if the government was defeated at the by-elections, a general election would be declared. Seán MacEntee accused MacBride of being pro-German during the war. MacBride denounced this assertion as a lie. On 18 October, MacBride accompanied by Noel Hartnett, handed in his nomination papers at Rathmines Town Hall. His proposer was Joseph P. Brennan, with Gerald McGowan the seconder.

In the lead-up to the election the Dáil was the scene of a heated debate on the sale of the well known Locke's distillery. The Taoiseach and some of his ministers came under attack. On 26 October, MacBride, speaking at Waterford, said that while he did not accuse ministers of fraud or bribery, they were subject to the influence of their political and personal friends in granting of licences, involving vast sums of money, to trading concerns. 'The costs of these concerns were not published and no information was made available to the public,' he said.

On voting day itself, 29 October, *The Irish Times* said, 'In the normal course of events, these by-elections would not be

of unusual importance; but the course of events is not normal.
The Taoiseach has made the result a matter of confidence.'

In MacBride's Dublin constituency the total electorate was
105,286, with a fifty three per cent turnout and a quota of
28,254 votes. The first preference votes cast were:

Mullins T.L.	Fianna Fáil	16,261
MacBride Seán	Clann na Poblachta	16,062
Rooney Eamon	Fine Gael	14,116
Dunne Seán	Labour	10,067

The second count resulted thus:

MacBride	21,755
Mullins	17,399
Rooney	15,361

The third and final count was:

MacBride	29,629
Mullins	20,197

On 31 October Mr de Valera announced that a general election would be held early in the following year. On 1 November
The Irish Times editorialised on the result:

> So far MacBride's group has not had much chance to build
> up a nation-wide organisation: but it has made a surprisingly
> good start. Its policy ... differs in few if any essentials from
> Fianna Fáil or Fine Gael; but it is an unhappy fact that
> there is still a section of the Irish community that will
> support any appeal to anti-British sentiment. The party's
> only merit is that in fact it represents something new;
> although its declared policy is as old as Sinn Féin, and its
> economic programme scarcely deserves to be taken seriously.
> It is a young party, led by a man with a political record of
> uncompromising Republicanism.

At a victory rally in Swords, MacBride said, 'the purpose of
Clann was to weld together those desirous of helping the
country in the present difficult times. In a short year the Party
has brought together the older people, who have taken the
opposite sides in Irish political life, and the younger people.'

MacBride entered Leinster House on 5 November 1947,

accompanied by his mother, to take his seat in Dáil Eireann. It was a highly-charged occasion for both of them. He was introduced to the Ceann Comhairle by Michael Donnellan TD, of Clann na Talmhan. MacBride was treated immediately in a hostile way by Fianna Fáil. He made his maiden speech the same day, speaking controversially on the sale of Locke's distillery. This distillery at Kilbeggan in Westmeath was being sold to foreign interests. A young TD from Laois-Offaly, Oliver J. Flanagan, had accused de Valera, Seán Lemass and Gerald Boland of bribery and corruption in the sale. MacBride said:

> I do not think that this inquiry ... will serve as a remedy. We have had inquiries before ... the question of granting or the withholding of a licence by a Department of State ... is done behind closed doors, there is no safeguard. It is done by the bureaucrat behind his closed doors, his iron curtain ... inquiries will not kill suspicion. A minister may not be a party to the abuse of powers but those who have the ear of the minister may well be ... I know nothing about these accusations.... A judicial tribunal should not be limited in function. I think Deputy Dillon's [an Independent TD] amendment is better worded.[2]

The Dáil decided on 7 November to set up a judicial inquiry into the matter, which would have power to summon all persons said to be involved.

On 7 November Frank Aiken said in the Dáil, 'I am delighted to see Deputy Dillon welcome with open arms and almost kissing the Kingstown Republican, who came in here the other day.' Dillon explained, 'Deputy MacBride and I were at school together under Fr. Sweetman.' Disorder ensued with General Mulcahy, Aiken, Donnellan, MacBride, Brendan Corish and the Speaker involved. Aiken defended his attack on MacBride by saying, 'His election address contained an allegation of corruption against the members of the government.'[3]

During the rest of that Dáil session to 15 December 1947, MacBride contributed more than sixty times to debate on items as diverse as fisheries, public health, hotels used as sanatoria, coal, currencies, forestry schemes, the International

Monetary Fund, partition, public libraries, railways, solicitors, taxes, the United Nations Organisation and prisoners. On prisoners he joined with the Labour leader, Mr Norton, requesting de Valera to ask the British authorities to release Irishmen in British prisons for Christmas. 'I feel if this were done by the Taoiseach, either in this House or through the other channels open to him, these men would be released.'

Clann na Poblachta elected a new executive on 30 November. Among those elected were: MacBride, Harnett, Con Lehane, Donal O'Donoghue, Jim Killeen, Peadar Cowan, The O'Rahilly, Roger McHugh, May Laverty, Mrs Maura Laverty, Mick Kelly, Tom Roycroft, Rory Brugha, Mick Ferguson, Austin Stack, Mick Fitzpatrick, Jack McQuillan and Tom Kenna.

On 11 December, James Dillon announced that he intended taking court action on the 1947 Health Act. He claimed that it was repugnant to the Constitution. He had in mind specifically Sections 21 and 28 which dealt with the mother and child services. These required the local health authorities to attend to the health of pupils at school, and for such medical inspections parents were obliged to submit their children.

Fianna Fáil had been in continuous office for sixteen years and the party's early revolutionary zeal had been dissipated by the practicalities of government. The Department of Finance controlled most government initiatives, and it was a cautious and even stultifying hand on national economic policy. The Department's pre-eminence went back to the early 1920s, when W.T. Cosgrave had an Irish-born official, C.J. Gregg, seconded from the Board of Inland Revenue in London to reorganise the Irish civil service. Gregg believed that the 'Treasury' should be paramount and he passed this view on to the Irish public service.[4]

The economic state of the country in 1947 was poor. Emigration and unemployment were high. The blizzard conditions of early 1947 led to a fuel supply crisis. Bread rationing was introduced. Yet workers felt that they were due increases in wages, following the sacrifices they had made during the Emergency. National teachers conducted an eight-month strike. Many of them were among the most ardent Fianna Fáil supporters. The teachers' stance was clear:

... the rise in the cost of living imposed great strain on their salaries. Small cost of living bonuses ... did nothing to alleviate distress. The INTO prepared new detailed salary and pension claims in 1945.... The government adopted an intransigent stance which resulted in the declaration of a strike from 20th march 1946. Even though the teachers' case had the support of the press and of parents' associations, the government remained adamant. At the request of the Archbishop of Dublin the teachers returned to their schools, defeated. For the government it could be regarded as something of a Pyrrhic victory and contributed to their losing office.[5]

Many teachers left Fianna Fáil and joined Clann na Poblachta.

De Valera was worried by the threat posed by Clann na Poblachta. After the reverses in the local elections, Fianna Fáil revised the Dáil constituencies, increasing the number of three-seat constituencies from fifteen to twenty-two. This would automatically help the largest party. The government also increased the number of Dáil seats from 138 to 147, despite a drop in the population. This done, de Valera decided to go to the country much earlier than was necessary.

On 19 December the Locke Tribunal reported that there was no foundation to charges laid against officials or politicians. Two days later de Valera, speaking at Oldcastle, County Meath, announced that there would be a general election early in February 1948. He said that 'a government of minority parties would have no purpose in common ... personal and party bargaining would take place on every important issue ... teamwork would be impossible.'

The political parties began to gear up for the election. The Clann would run three candidates in Dublin South West; MacBride, Miss May Laverty and Dr Batterberry; Noel Hartnett and Dr J.P. Brennan were selected for Dun Laoghaire. On 23 December *The Irish Times* announced that 'Dr N. Browne, assistant medical superintendent of Newcastle Sanatorium will contest Dublin South East as a candidate for Clann na Poblachta'. MacBride suggested that there was nothing in the Constitution to preclude the Six-County MPs from being invited to sit in the Dáil. De Valera ridiculed this.

Seán MacEntee, speaking at a selection convention in
Dublin South East, attacked the Clann. He said:

There were political parties in this country, in which Communists played a very large part. The Irish Labour Party
was undoubtedly one of them and Clann na Poblachta was
an organisation which, if published declarations meant
anything, had associated with it men and women who were
communistic in everything except their acceptance of the
name. Some of them had been in Saor Eire, others in the
Republican Congress and others in the Vanguard move-
ments, all definitely Communistic Organisations.[6]

De Valera knew that Clann na Poblachta was still trying to
establish a national organisation. It had its first national
conference in December 1947, the same month the election
was announced; 372 delegates arrived from 252 branches.
This was not a sound platform to contest the coming election.
The campaign was a vigorous one, with Fianna Fáil concentrat-
ing its main criticism on Clann na Poblachta and in particular
on MacBride. The Clann nominated 93 candidates, more than
any other party except Fianna Fáil. But its organisation was
not strong enough to sustain such a commitment of candidates.
It put forward a very broad policy which incorporated the
Bishop of Clonfert's social policy.

Dr Dignan, the bishop of Clonfert, a Fianna Fáil supporter,
had been made Chairman of the National Insurance Society
in the early 1940s by the Minister for Health, Seán MacEntee.
In October 1944 the bishop issued a paper, 'Social Security:
outlines of a scheme of a national health insurance'. This
followed closely Catholic teaching, which MacEntee ostensibly
wanted to implement. Yet to Dignan's consternation and to
the merriment of MacEntee's own cabinet colleagues, MacEntee rejected the proposals in an almost virulent way. He
claimed the state could not afford such a scheme even if it was
desirable, which he believed it was not. Dignan asked, 'Does
the Minister mean that a social and economic system based on
these principles is impracticable in Ireland?' He then attacked
the existing social services as unChristian, belittling the
dignity of people, just like the Poor Law legislation of the past.
When the bishop's tenure of office as chairman was up in

1945, MacEntee did not reappoint him. Clann na Poblachta's adoption of the bishop's Catholic social proposals was partly a ploy to offset a communistic smear, attempted on it by MacEntee.

The Dublin South Central branch of the Clann issued a poster outlining its policies. These included the elimination of jobbery, political preferment and corruption from public life. It called for a social and economic system based on Christian principles and a comprehensive social insurance scheme on the basis of the plan drawn up by 'Most Rev. Dignan, Bishop of Clonfert'. It looked for full employment, the abolition of slums, reduction in the cost of living and the provision of sanitoria for those afflicted with tuberculosis. The school leaving age was to be raised to sixteen with free education for all up to university level. Lastly it proclaimed the necessity for freedom and independence for all Ireland as a democratic republic.

Fianna Fáil were very worried and the smearing continued with MacBride being referred to as a gunman. Louie O'Brien recalls one of the stories recounting that wherever MacBride went in public, he would be followed closely by Noel Hartnett, who would be followed by Donal O'Donoghue. The story line describing who the trio were, went thus: 'Hartnett was the shadow of the gunman and O'Donoghue was the shadow of the shadow of the gunman'.

Noel Browne first met MacBride in late 1947 when they travelled to Ealing Studios in London where the Clan were making a first ever election film. He has described MacBride as: 'Of medium height, round-shouldered, he looked frail, indeed positively consumptive.... Overall he had a gaunt, cadaverous appearance and his sallow complexion gave him a Mediterranean look. His curved crescent-shaped nose suggested a distinctly Middle Eastern appearance, and left an impression on foreigners.'[7]

MacBride began to receive wider recognition. *The Observer* newspaper wrote of him on 18 January 1948:

MacBride has caught hold of the popular imagination, and his chances of a real victory in the February General Election are heatedly discussed in every Dublin bar. Aged forty-three, smooth not to say slick in manner, an engaging and plausible talker with Latin features. His following is composed of extreme chauvinists or incorrigible Celts, disgruntled I.R.A., a few ex-communists, and some political adventurers. His success was probably due to the suffering of the working and middle classes now, as Irish prices steadily rise, and his anti-British line is always a good card to play in popular electioneering.

The Clann's candidates were 23 shopkeepers, 19 teachers, 13 lawyers, 10 doctors, 13 farmers, and 12 with no stated profession.

Brian Inglis covered the general election for *The Irish Times*. He attended MacBride's first meeting of his nationwide tour in Ballina, County Mayo, and wished MacBride well. Inglis thought him refined and modest compared to most Irish politicians, but he found that MacBride 'was not impressive on the platform. His face, skull-like in its contours, split rather than relaxed by his rare smile, was a little intimidating: and the foreign inflection was not as attractive on the hustings as it could be in conversation. He spoke without relish or subtlety of … the repatriation of Ireland's assets and afforestation. MacBride tried to stop his supporters shouting "Up MacBride" which might have made his well attended meetings less dull and prosaic. The lack of finance and sufficient party workers became apparent early on in the campaign….' Inglis added, 'it quickly became obvious that MacBride did not have the personality needed to create a revolution in voting habits.'[8]

The election result was Fianna Fáil 68, Fine Gael 31, Labour 14, Clann na Poblachta 10, Clann na Talmhan 7, National Labour 5, Others 12. Although Clann na Poblachta won the third highest number of votes, it got a poor return in seats. Proportionally it deserved nineteen seats. Ten of its candidates just failed to gain the last seat in the multi-seat constituencies; forty-seven others lost their deposits. The Clann secured ten seats from 175,000 votes, while Fine Gael secured thirty-one seats from 262,000 votes. It was a major disappointment for MacBride and his party given the euphoria of the campaign. But, bearing in mind the party's brief political existence, it was an electoral success of considerable proportions.

Fianna Fáil, though still the largest single party in the Dáil, had lost its overall majority. De Valera was adamant that Fianna Fáil would not join a coalition, nor ask any other party for support. But, as in 1932, he expected to gain support and remain in power. The five National Labour Party TDs and a few Independents were expected to back Fianna Fáil. De Valera never expected that the motley opposition parties could come together to form a government. That however is precisely what they did, due to their great dislike of him.

The main stumbling-block was the leader of Fine Gael, Richard Mulcahy. He had been a tough Minister for Defence in the old Cumann na nGaedheal government and was the Free State Army leader during the Civil War. Seán MacBride could not agree to him becoming Taoiseach. MacBride had a difficult enough time selling to his own party the idea of coalition with their former bitter enemies. Among those who left the party on the issue was Seán South of Limerick. Mulcahy, an honourable man, made way for John A. Costello, a former Attorney General in the Cosgrave government and a fellow barrister with MacBride, to become Taoiseach of a new inter-party government. MacBride became Minister for External Affairs and he nominated his 32-year old colleague, Noel Browne, to become Minister for Health on his first day in Dáil Eireann.

Mulcahy became Minister for Education. Joe Blowick, the leader of Clann na Talmhan, became Minister for Lands. James Dillon, an Independent, was made Minister for Agriculture. Patrick McGilligan and Dan Morrissey of Fine Gael got Finance and Industry and Commerce respectively. William Norton, the leader of the Labour Party, became Tánaiste and Minister for Social Welfare.

MacBride's own governmental colleagues understood the pressures he was under and responded favourably without his intervention. On the day the government was formed, the new Minister for Defence, General Seán MacEoin, called to Roebuck House and told MacBride that he had Costello's agreement to release the remaining republican prisoners from Portlaoise jail.

Among those released was the son of the famous Lord Mayor of Cork, also called Tomas MacCurtain, whom MacBride had saved from hanging in 1941. Another was Harry White, whom MacBride had also saved from execution after being found guilty of murder and sentenced to death in 1946. Another prisoner freed was Brendan Behan. MacBride was very proud of the fact that the Coalition Government was the first government since 1922 to hold no political prisoners.

MacBride had two main demands for a government programme. He wanted a vigorous afforestation campaign and a major cash input from the Irish Hospitals Sweepstakes for the provision of sanatoria for the eradication of tuberculosis. On the motion to elect the Taoiseach in the Dáil on 18 February 1948, MacBride said:

> In the election, the people voted by 750,000 to 500,000 votes clearly indicating that they wished to terminate the virtual political monopoly which has existed for some 16 years. That was the clear direction to this Parliament.... All parties in this House are unanimous in their desire to reunite the nation and to undo Partition.... There are a number of urgent problems ... emigration, rural depopulation, the fall in agricultural production, tuberculosis.... The ultimate political objective of the Party which I have the honour to represent in this House, is the reintegration of the nation as a republic, free from any association with any other country.... We cannot claim in this Election we secured a mandate from the people which would enable us to repeal, or seek to repeal the External Relations Act.... This therefore has to remain in abeyance for the time being.... I trust that the other parties in this House will see the wisdom of pursuing such a policy.

Very shortly after this, the Taoiseach was speaking publicly about the repeal of the External Relations Act. Fine Gael had decided that never again would Fianna Fáil and de Valera lay claim to be the only republican party.

Patrick Keatinge has written that the relationship between Costello and MacBride was not that of a senior and junior partner. He says that the exigencies of the coalition government made it difficult for Costello to exert the normal authority of a head of government. Keatinge adds, 'although MacBride

Maud holds her new-born baby son at her Paris home, February 1904.
Alongside is the baby's father, Major John MacBride. The flag is that of
the Irish Brigade from the Boer War. (Courtesy of Seán MacBride Estate)

Maud holds baby Seán in Dublin for his christening, April 1904.
(Courtesy of Seán MacBride Estate)

Collection Costey   COLLEVILLE-sur-MER. - Villa des Mouettes

Les Moettes Coleville Normandy. This house was purchased in 1903 by Maud as a summer retreat. It was much frequented by Yeats in subsequent years. (Courtesy of Seán MacBride Estate)

Infant Seán, Maud, and Iseult in 1905.
(Courtesy of Seán MacBride Estate)

First communion souvenir with Seán's surname given as Gonne, 1911.
(Courtesy of Seán MacBride Estate)

*After Papal audience in April 1911. Barry O'Delaney, a long-time
associate of Maud's, Seagan and Maud.
(Courtesy of Seán MacBride Estate)*

*On the steps of St. Peter's Basilica Rome at 3 p.m. on 3 April 1911. Barry
O'Delaney and Seagan.
(Courtesy of Seán MacBride Estate)*

Seagan as a mass server.
(Courtesy of Seán MacBride Estate)

*Seagan rowing a boat, accompanied by Barry O'Delaney (below), on the
lake in the Bois de Boulogne, Paris, 23 September 1916.
(Courtesy of Seán MacBride Estate)*

Portrait of Maud as a young woman.
(Courtesy of Seán MacBride Estate)

Seán as a youth.
(Courtesy of Louie O' Brien)

Catalina Bulfin in 1926, the year
of her marriage.
(Courtesy of Anna MacBride-White)

Seán as a young man.
(Courtesy of Louie O' Brien)

Seán with his daughter Anna on holiday in Glengarriff,
June 1937. (Courtesy of Louie O' Brien)

Seán in the garden of his home, Roebuck House, Clonskeagh, Dublin, in the late 1930s.

The family at home in Roebuck, 1947. From left, Maud Gonne, Anna, Seán, Tiernan and Kid MacBride. (Courtesy of Louie O' Brien)

Portrait of Seán MacBride, 1948. (Courtesy of Louie O' Brien)

At a friend's farm. Included in the photo are: Margaret Burke Sheridan, Kid MacBride and Anna MacBride-White.

At a lecture given by the Minister for External Affairs, Mr. Seán MacBride, to members of the Clann na Poblachta Party at Clery's Ballroom, Dublin. Left to right: The O'Rahilly; the Minister; Mr. D. Guilfoyle and Mrs. L. O'Brien, 1949. (Courtesy of Louie O'Brien)

Seán with members of Clann na Poblachta in the early 1950s. (Courtesy of Tiernan MacBride)

Geneva, early 1960s, Seán MacBride with his Irish staff at International Commission of Jurists.
(Courtesy of Máireann McHugh)

Kid MacBride outside Roebuck House in the early 1970s.

Roebuck House (Photograph by author)

Seán at the unveiling of "Tribute Head" donated by artists for Amnesty, on 26 June 1983, South African Freedom Day, in the twentieth year of the imprisonment of Nelson Mandela, Merrion Square, Dublin. (Photograph by author)

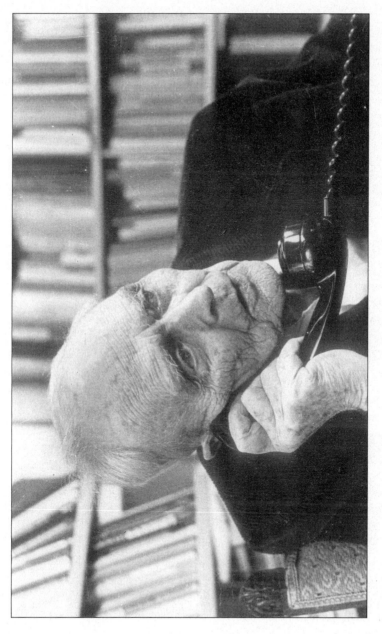

Above and on following pages – previously unpublished photos of Seán MacBride taken shortly before his death (Courtesy of Bill Doyle)

Anna MacBride-White and Tiernan MacBride, Seán's two children, in 1991. (Photograph by author)

Tiernan MacBride shows a walking stick of his grandfather, Major John MacBride, at the launch of *Major John MacBride, 1865-1916* to Tony Jordan (the author) and Anna MacBride-White. (Courtesy of *The Irish Times*)

was not the policy-maker, he was in a position to exert more influence than might have been otherwise the case. The fact that the two men had been colleagues at the bar prior to their term in power, and that Costello had been instrumental in bringing MacBride into parliamentary politics may well have facilitated the relationship.'9

W.B. Yeats's body had lain interred in France during the war. The time had come to bring it home for burial in Sligo where the poet had wished to lie. Seán MacBride, as Minister for External Affairs, organised the return of Yeats's body. On 25 August 1948, the Irish naval service corvette, *Macha*, left Dun Laoghaire for Nice. There, as the coffin was brought aboard, draped with the Irish tricolour, the Irish and French national anthems were played. A Mentone lawyer, Mr Otto, read a poem in French dedicated to Yeats.

As the *Macha* sailed for home, it was made clear that it would have to dock at Galway instead of Sligo, where there were insufficient facilities. Sligo Corporation protested and sent a telegram to the Minister for Defence.

The State had intended to afford the remains a state funeral but, in deference to the poet's family, the only state ceremonial was the provision of a military guard of honour for the body as it arrived in Sligo.

A veil of mist hung over the bare head of Ben Bulben as the remains arrived in Sligo from Galway by motor hearse. Soft grey rain swept in from the sea at Drumcliffe as the tricolour-covered plain wooden coffin was laid to rest near the little parish church. Seán MacBride represented the government at the ceremony. He was also representing his mother, who was too weak to journey to Sligo. She was happy that Willie Yeats had found his requested resting place. MacBride, of course, was there on his own behalf, too, for among the large gathering, he probably had known Yeats the longest.

14

Minister for External Affairs

The new inter-party government was breaking ground and took some time to settle down and master their various portfolios. John A. Costello also took time to establish his authority in cabinet. The civil service, and particularly the Department of Finance under T.J. McGelligott, intended to get control of the ministers as quickly as possible. Their main opponent in the early days of the new government was Seán MacBride, who bombarded the cabinet with memoranda on almost every issue before it. Although his brief was External Affairs, he got involved in all aspects of economic development. Maurice Moynihan was the secretary to the Taoiseach and as such secretary to the government. As de Valera had been for such a long time his own Minister for External Affairs, Moynihan had been used to exercising great control over that department too. MacBride did not trust him and Moynihan only attended the first two meetings of the new government. Liam Cosgrave or Costello himself were in the habit of taking notes of decisions arrived at in cabinet.[1]

A political comment made by Seán Lemass while speaking in 1949 on bilateral and multilateral trade policy, was undisguised, 'there is perhaps a suspicion in some quarters that the Minister for External Affairs acts in these matters independently of his colleagues or even in conflict with them'.[2] Later, in 1951, de Valera asked MacBride, 'which was the driving department ... charged with looking after the thing [the interdepartmental foreign trade committee] as a whole, to push it definitively?' MacBride replied, 'by and large it is all centred in the Department of External Affairs, but you always have conflicting interests ... between the Department of Agriculture,

Industry and Commerce and very often the Department of Finance. By maintaining a policy of neutrality and by trying to provide a good service, the Department of External Affairs exercises a good deal of influence.'[3]

Ronan Fanning clearly indicates that this was indeed so, in his major study of the Department of Finance. He points out that MacBride's two major demands on the formation of the government centred on that department, as he demanded money for afforestation, and money for Health, via the Hospital Sweepstakes. Fanning adds that those in that department who had kept an eye on MacBride's public pronouncements on fiscal matters in previous years, would have viewed his accession to government with some trepidation. This was soon justified. Fanning writes:

> An inspection of Finances archives, reveals an explosive growth in the volume of records from 1946-47 onwards and a notable feature of this development is how much of this additional documentation came from the Department of External Affairs. Another index of that department's new power and confidence was its insistence that all negotiations between Irish governmental departments and their British counterparts should be conducted under its auspices and that the practice of direct negotiations should cease.[4]

MacBride gave himself over totally to his role in government and demanded the same from the civil servants in his department and the diplomats in overseas postings. He enjoyed the life of the international negotiator, mixing with world leaders the likes of Attlee, Monnet, Schuman and Truman. He no longer questioned the loyalty of civil servants, but he remained sceptical about their expertise and vision on the necessary economic expansion required to raise the living standards of the Irish people.

MacBride's heavy demands on the civil servants in his department, particularly those who were called upon to serve their country abroad was acknowledged in a speech in the Dáil in 1951. He expected them to follow his own example:

> It is essential, probably more essential in the Department of External Affairs than in any other Department, that the officers should be imbued with a spirit of national self-

responsibility. They have to be prepared to work harder than in other Departments, to make personal sacrifices, even heavy sacrifices, in order to discharge their duties to this nation effectively. Most officers in the Department, but particularly those who serve abroad, have to develop a sense of initiative and a sense of devotion to duty which is not called for to the same extent from civil servants who work at home in the larger departments.... Each individual member of our staff abroad ... has to represent this nation for twenty-four hours around the clock. Every action of his may bring credit or discredit on this nation because he or she will be looked upon as the representative of this nation. By their actions and by their zeal to duty we will be judged abroad.[5]

In the late 1930s MacBride had met de Valera many times to urge afforestation. A large forestry programme was envisioned in the Banking and Currency Commission in 1938, but de Valera deferred to the Department of Finance, which maintained that forestry was too expensive and could never become a short-term economic proposition.

MacBride was given the cabinet responsibility for post-war Marshall Aid and the European Economic Recovery Programme Plan. A formal plan had to be presented to the Organisation for European Economic Cooperation (OEEC), through which the American government had decided to channel all Marshall Aid. MacBride was appointed negotiator for the entire sixteen-country group. He got American support for the idea that the aid should be used to encourage growth, and not merely for short-term purposes. MacBride produced the Long-Term Recovery Programme, published in January 1949, which was required to qualify for Marshall Aid.

'His influence was further enhanced by his friendship with Averell Harriman, the European Ambassador at Large for the European Cooperation Agreement, with whom he acted as a sort of unofficial representative of the council of Ministers, and by his even closer friendship with the American Minister to Ireland, George Garrett, with whom he regularly shared a frugal lunch of poached eggs on toast in his office in Iveagh House.'[6]

Speaking on these matters in the Dáil MacBride said:

The Economic Recovery Plan emerged as a result of a
speech made by the United States Secretary of State,
General Marshall, in June 1947. Following upon the War,
a tremendous amount of economic destruction as well as
material destruction had occurred. The Economic Recovery
Plan, as I conceive it, is intended to remove, as far as
possible, the motive of economic rivalry and economic
domination, and to make available the resources of Europe,
on a basis of mutual help to try to develop a sense of co-
operation between the nations of Europe and the Western
hemisphere.... Our financial and currency system has been
linked with the Sterling area. [MacBride tried, without
success, to get cabinet approval to break the link with
Sterling.] To a large extent, our savings and our money
have been put in the bank around the corner. The bank
around the corner is now in some grave difficulties, so far
as converting its assets into dollars or hard currency is
concerned.... It may be difficult to understand why in the
case of Ireland, Aid by way of grant, was not forthcoming.
We do not complain of it. We have no claim on it. It is
entirely a matter for them [the US Congress]....In America
and Britain, I found there was a completely erroneous
impression as to the standard of living of our people....
There were no shortages.[7]

MacBride's views on economics drew a variety of criticism:

Another minister Lemass constantly castigated for his
allegedly shallow economic views was Seán MacBride, the
Minister for Foreign Affairs. MacBride, in particular, had
sought to focus attention on Ireland's external assets. Due
to two world wars, in which her volume of imports contracted
far more than her volume of exports, Ireland had accumu-
lated substantial external assets. Gradually Costello,
McGilligan, Lemass and responsible opinion in general
moved towards acceptance of the principle of repatriation
of external assets if the use found for them at home was as
productive as elsewhere. This, of course, was horribly difficult to ensure. In the meantime there was no question of

any general repatriation. The flurry of speeches on this issue was in a sense a distraction. For while Costello, McGilligan and Lemass might unite in castigating Mac-Bride's economic naïveté, the fact was that — as Lemass later openly admitted — the Fianna Fáil spokesman, at least, had no positive programme to advance.[8]

MacBride's Long-term Recovery Programme envisaged the planting of 10,000 hectares of new forest per annum over forty years, resulting in a state forest of 470,000 hectares in 1990. The Department of Finance fought him every inch of the way and succeeded in thwarting these aims.

'The MacBride Expansion', as it might be called, was a positive move in the direction of a long-term forest programme. 'It represented the first major change of forest policy at government level since the State had come into being, and it brought ancillary, far reaching, though seldom acknowledged, consequences in its wake … perhaps easier for him that at least some of the civil servants with whom he dealt abrasively on the issue were not of his own department.… It was with the civil servants of Finance and Lands, not Foreign Affairs, that MacBride crossed swords over forestry.'[9] MacBride had tried to have the Marshall Aid funds paid as a grant, rather than as a loan. But the Americans refused, principally because they saw no Communist threat in Ireland. The Department of Finance was against receiving Marshall Aid. It believed that the politicians would spend it foolishly and would have to pay it back later. Marshall Aid was a godsend for the government's investment programme. It accounted for 50 per cent of the total inter-party investment. MacBride had sought a £120 million grant, but got less than £50 million.

The civil service and much of the cabinet had little investment or expansionary experience. Most of the grant was spent on land rehabilitation, electricity supply, telephones and forestry. MacBride tried to get cabinet approval to build new factories and rent them to private manufacturing companies. This was refused. One of the successes of the inter-party government was the setting up of the Industrial Development Company (IDA) in 1949, and Córas Tráchtála (the Irish Export Board) in 1952, which in time would develop many of

MacBride's ideas about industrialisation and development. The Department of Finance opposed these two new bodies, in part because MacBride was such an ardent supporter. In time the Minister for Finance, Patrick McGilligan, got the measure of his officials. He had to because their bête noire, MacBride, began to spend more and more time out of the country.

Another success of the government was a tenfold increase in building local authority houses from 1,108 in 1947 to 11,305 in 1951. The Department of Finance and the Central Bank had not been accustomed to the principle of borrowing for capital projects. The inertia was to be gradually overcome. The idea of long-term economic aims developed and their implementation was pursued with some vigour. John A. Murphy has written: 'the beginnings of economic planning are to be found in this first Coalition period, predating by seven years T.K. Whittaker's famous memorandum ... which is still popularly believed to be the point of departure for Government Economic Planning'.[10]

The British and Americans were pleasantly surprised that MacBride was facing up so well to the Realpolitik of international affairs. MacBride had even expelled one of his own party members, Peadar Cowan, for voting against the US Dollar Loan in the Dáil. In the summer of 1948 Clement Attlee, the British Prime Minister, visited Dublin to sign the Anglo-Irish Trade Agreement. He subsequently took his family on a holiday to County Mayo, where he spent some time in MacBride's company. Attlee felt there could be some movement on partition, but he told MacBride that the Labour Party could not act alone. He promised to set up a dinner party where he and MacBride could meet Churchill, the leader of the opposition, to discuss the North. MacBride saw the Attlee family off at Collinstown airport. Attlee said that he had thoroughly enjoyed his visit and the very warm welcome he got on his travels. Cordial relations with Britain continued when a British naval group visited Irish ports.

Attlee invited MacBride to London to meet Churchill over dinner. It did not prove to be a happy encounter. 'I believe your father and I were both in South Africa in 1900, but on different sides,' Churchill said. MacBride concurred. 'It appears you and I were both at the Anglo-Irish Conference in 1921, but on

opposite sides. It seems we are fated to be always adversaries.'
MacBride again agreed. 'So much the better, because on the
Irish question, I have my loyalties. I cannot let down my
Unionist friends in Ulster,' Churchill said, ending his partici-
pation in the conversation.[11]

15

Irish Republic

The inter-party government's single most important act was the Declaration of an Irish Republic. This appears to have been a Fine Gael initiative, though MacBride was party to it. The Fianna Fáil government had earlier been negotiating with the British on a nationality code and law. MacBride discovered that, under that code, Irish people were described as 'Commonwealth' citizens. This alarmed him, for if Ireland left the Commonwealth, Irish citizens could be disadvantaged in Britain. He successfully reviewed these matters with the British and safeguarded the rights of Irish citizens, regardless of the Commonwealth. Most of the cabinet believed that the External Relations Act of 1936 would have to be repealed. The British sovereign was an anomaly.

James Dillon was deputy leader of Fine Gael under W.T. Cosgrave. He resigned from the party in 1942, after he opposed neutrality. He was a noted orator. In July 1945 Dillon had asked de Valera to declare his view of the constitutional status of the State. Referring to the written Constitution of 1937, de Valera quoted five reference dictionaries on the definition of a republic, trying to demonstrate that the Irish Free State was indeed a republic. He explained away the 1936 External Relations Act by which the monarch acted on behalf of the government, for the purpose of appointing diplomatic and consular representatives and the conclusion of international agreements, as a 'simple statute repealable by the legislature and not a fundamental law'. In answer to the question 'Are we or are we not a member of the British Commonwealth?' de Valera said, 'It depends on what the essential element is, in the Constitution of the British Commonwealth.

His Majesty's government said in 1937, "that they are prepared to treat the new Constitution as not affecting a fundamental alteration in the position of the Irish Free State — as a member of the British Commonwealth of Nations".'[1]

A British Commonwealth Conference was pending. John Costello was invited, but MacBride advised him not to go. He said in the Dáil on 20 July 1948: 'The Crown and outworn forms that belong to British Constitutional history are merely reminders of an unhappy past we want to bury.' On the following day MacBride, in answer to a Dáil question said: 'We are certainly not a member of the British Commonwealth of Nations.' One week later, Costello himself said: 'The constitutional position is that Ireland is a sovereign, independent democratic state associated with the members of the British Commonwealth ... the process by which Ireland ceased formally to be a member of the Commonwealth has been one of gradual development.' In August William Norton, the Tánaiste, declared: 'It would do our national self-respect good both at home and abroad, if we were to proceed without delay to abolish the External Relations Act.' De Valera replied, 'Go ahead. You will get no opposition from us.'[2]

In September 1948 Costello went on a Canadian tour. While there he encountered irritating protocol difficulties over toasts to the King and the President of Ireland. In Ireland, the *Sunday Independent* wrote an apparently inspired story that Ireland was to declare itself a Republic and repeal the External Relations Act. 'There is a suspicion that MacBride gave Costello's speech to the Canadian Bar Association his imprimatur, because he mistakenly believed that it heralded the official announcement of the repeal of the Act, and then prompted the Irish newspapers with an advance release of the speech through the Department of External Affairs.'[3] MacBride telegrammed Costello not to comment on the story at a forthcoming press conference, but Costello did confirm that he intended to repeal the Act.

The Irish newspapers, which were relying on agency reports from Canada, gave the announcement front page treatment. They emphasised that in Costello's word, the Act was to be 'scrapped'. As Ian McCabe writes, this 'effectively made it impossible for the Irish government to backtrack and survive'.[4]

Whether the cabinet had formally agreed to such a move is debated, though Ian McCabe's research would tend to suggest it was not.[5]

When MacBride was taking over at Iveagh House, he asked Louie O'Brien to go into the department with him as an unpaid secretary. He told her that after sixteen years of Fianna Fáil rule, most of the officials there were probably de Valera supporters, and enemies of his. He would need somebody he could trust to handle sensitive matters. She and others in the department were horrified when they got forewarning of the *Sunday Independent* article. MacBride too appeared to be aghast, as it was clear there must have been a cabinet leak. 'We suffered from the same shock as Costello was suffering from over there in Canada. The wires between Canada and Ireland lit up that night, as Costello sought advice from Dublin,' she says. It was only after several years that she discovered, by chance and through a third party, that MacBride himself had been responsible for the leak. Though she remained on with MacBride and continued to live at Roebuck House on a paying basis for the next thirty years, she has written: 'It was the first glimpse I got of the feet of clay! So many dishonest and dishonourable acts followed with the years that I became totally disillusioned.'[6]

On his arrival home at Cobh on 1 October 1948, MacBride welcomed Costello and congratulated him on his statement in Canada. The dye was cast. In his book *The Formulation of Irish Foreign Policy*, Patrick Keatinge writes:

> Mr Costello's government relied for its survival on the active support of the new Clann na Poblachta party which had enjoyed some success at the polls. In return, that party's leader, Mr Seán MacBride, obtained the portfolio of External Affairs. Unlike Costello, he did advocate a clear alternative to external association, for he had fought a vigorous campaign largely on the issue of breaking with the Commonwealth and proclaiming a Republic. His views could not therefore be taken lightly and indeed, found ready public support, from other prominent members of the relatively loose coalition government. Under these circumstances, there could be no return to positive mem-

bership of the Commonwealth, and Mr Costello abandoned
this traditional aim of his own party and declared the
Republic, retaining some semblance of independence by
publicly announcing the policy, without prior notice and
when outside the country.[7]

Garret FitzGerald has written with some unhappiness of
these events. He had canvassed for John A. Costello in the
Dublin South East constituency in the 1948 election. He writes:

> My understanding was that Fine Gael supported Common-
> wealth membership, and Joan and I canvassed accordingly:
> we particularly remember reassuring the inhabitants of
> Waterloo Road on the point. After the election ... MacBride
> became Minister for External Affairs. I still recall my dis-
> illusionment at this development. I had been brought up to
> regard MacBride with deep hostility; a member of the IRA
> from the Civil War onwards, he had been its chief of staff in
> the mid-30s just after some particularly shocking murders
> had made a profound impression on me, including one near
> Ring College when I was at school there. His later conversion
> to constitutionalism had seemed to me ambivalent ... My
> unhappiness was intensified when, ... the Taoiseach
> announced the Government's intension to declare a republic
> ... At that time this clearly meant leaving the Common-
> wealth, for the evolution of which into a body of sovereign,
> independent states John Costello, as Attorney General,
> with people like my father, Paddy McGilligan, and Kevin
> O'Higgins, had worked so successfully in the years before
> 1932. Moreover, in the months that followed that announce-
> ment the Government also decided not to join NATO ...
> I attributed the dynamic of this decision to MacBride
> also.[8]

Later in October MacBride attended the Chequers Commonwealth Conference as an observer. He received support
for his government's stance from several Commonwealth
leaders, including the prime ministers of New Zealand,
Australia and Canada.

On 17 November 1948 the Repeal of the External Relations
Act was introduced in the Dáil. John Costello said:

This Bill is a simple Bill but it has tremendous and, I believe and hope, very beneficial results. The first section repeals the External Relations Act.... The name of the State is Ireland and the description of the State is the Republic of Ireland.... Diplomatic representatives will be received by the President of Ireland, the Head of State.... This Bill if it is passed unanimously will I believe ... bring peace here in this part of our country and by bringing this country well on to the international stage, by lifting this problem of Partition from the domestic arena and putting it on to the international scene, give us not a faint hope but a clear prospect of bringing about the unity of Ireland. There have been smug, fearsome declarations by British Ministers that the problem of Partition is an Irish problem, that must be settled by Irishmen. The problem was created by an Act of the British Parliament, the Government of Ireland Act 1920 ... and it is for them to solve the problem. That 1920 Act was put on the Statute Book and brought into operation without a single vote cast in favour by any Irish representative in the British Parliament, or without anybody North or South wanting it. The problem of undoing the wrongdoing, devolves upon the British Government. We are doing our part down here.[9]

During MacBride's contribution to the debate, he clashed with de Valera's earlier approach to the republic and his dictionary attempts to show that Ireland was a republic despite having the British sovereign as head of the state for external affairs purposes.

The following brief extract from the debate is interesting in itself, but all the more so when we realise that at that stage, the pupil and ex-disciple had turned the tables on his master and hero.

Mr de Valera: I did not want to have a controversy on words.

Mr MacBride: Kindly refrain from interrupting when I am speaking. You took it in very bad humour when I interrupted a few minutes ago. You must allow me to conclude. That was in November, 1938. But then we had another speech, reported also in the *Irish Press*, in December, 1938, in which again he was dealing with the question of a republic and said:

> I for one am sorry, because I feel that if we were able to say we are an independent republic there would be none of this confusion which exists at the moment which is helping to cause dissatisfaction and is, in a sense, a source of danger.

Accordingly, in 1938 Deputy de Valera thought he was not able to say that we were an independent republic and that if he had been able to say we were an independent republic there would have been no confusion; that the confusion that did exist then was in his view a source of danger and was helping to cause dissatisfaction. That was in 1938. We had no republic then, according to Deputy de Valera, but all that we had to do was to repeal this Act in order to have it. Deputy de Valera, apparently, when he indulges in justification, suffers from a short memory in this matter. A few years later Deputy de Valera came into these benches here, escorted by some of his officials carrying dictionaries, and, lo and behold, we had a republic out of the dictionaries, though in 1938 we had no republic.

Mr de Valera: Because the State has every characteristic of a republic.

Mr MacBride: All right. If you want to ask questions and interrupt, let me ask this: What happened between December, 1938, and the date when you came in with your dictionaries to change the position?

Mr de Valera: What happened was this, if I might answer the question. When I was asked to give an authoritative statement, I gave it and proved it.

Mr MacBride: Therefore, you thought you were at liberty in 1938 to go around making untrue statements about the republic?

Mr de Valera: In 1938 I knew there were people who, no matter what I said to them, were not going to be convinced, just the same as there are people at the present time who will not be convinced.

Mr MacBride: Therefore, you thought you could go to the Ard-Fheis and tell them something that was untrue, tell them that we had not a republic and keep it locked up in your heart until 1946, when you came in here with dictionaries.

Mr de Valera: Not at all. There was a misunderstanding of the effect of the External Relations Act. I knew the simplest way to deal with the argument was to satisfy those people who would not be satisfied by my view of it. There was one way in which it could be done and, because it is being done to clear the confusion, that is the only reason why I am voting for the Bill.

Mr MacBride: All right. In 1938 you created confusion in the public mind by telling the Ard-Fheis and the people at large:

> I for one am sorry because I feel that if we were able to say we are an independent republic there would be none of the confusion which exists at the moment...

Having deliberately created confusion in 1938, then it was necessary to bring in dictionaries in 1946 to undo the confusion created by the Leader of the Opposition then. I leave that to the people to judge whether it makes sense or not. It is all a misunderstanding on his side.

Now, I said that we had a head of State and that we had not a head of State for external purposes. As the House knows, the credentials of Ambassadors and Ministers are signed by the head of State. Every single credential issued by the Leader of the Opposition, while he occupied my present position, for an Ambassador or a Minister, was signed by the King of Britain, was sent over by the Deputy and signed by the King. We had a President in the Park, and I am not aware that he signed any credentials. Was I misleading the House when I said that we had a head of State and we had not a head of State? The Leader of the Opposition thinks that by reading words and talking about statutory instruments, organs, and statutory agents he is able to confuse the people sufficiently to prevent the people from appreciating what the position in fact was. You only have to read the Act, you only have to understand the facts, to understand that from 1936, while the Leader of the Opposition was in my office, he utilised the King of Britain as Head of State for external affairs.

Mr de Valera: I deny that I used him as head of State. It is quite untrue.

Mr MacBride: Do you deny having sent the credentials for Ambassadors and Ministers to be signed by the King?

Mr de Valera: I sent —

Mr MacBride: Answer that first.

Mr de Valera: I will answer the question that requires to be answered.

Mr MacBride: Very well, if you are not prepared to answer the question, do not interrupt.

Mr de Valera: I am not in the witness box. The Minister had better not try that sort of thing on me.

An Leas-Cheann Comhairle: I suggest that if we had less of the second person it would be better. We have had too much of it.

Mr MacBride: If there is any doubt about it I will produce evidence in this House to show that the Leader of the Opposition used the King of Britain as head of the State.

Mr de Valera: I deny that I used the King of Britain as head of the State. I used him in accordance with the Act as a statutory agent to put his name to a document which I had written.

Mr MacBride: A few minutes ago there was no King in the Act.

Mr de Valera: There was no King of Ireland in that Act. You are playing with words.

Captain Cowan: Was that King an Irish citizen?

Mr de Valera: We could have used the President of the United States just as well.

Mr S. Collins: Why did you not?

Mr MacBride: All right. We have heard a lot about the President of the United States. It is quite true that there is no reference in the Constitution of the United States to the Republic of the United States of America, but then the United States of America do not go and use the King of another country to sign their heads of States treaties or to accredit their Ambassadors and Ministers.

Mr de Valera: I want the truth.

Mr MacBride: That is true.

Mr de Valera: You are misrepresenting in every word the real situation.

Mr MacBride: I will produce the evidence of it if the Deputy denies it.

Mr de Valera: I would like to see you try to prove it in any reasonable court.

Mr MacBride: The letters of credence have been signed the whole time through by the King of Britain at the request of the Deputy. Surely he is not trying to deny that.

Mr de Valera: I do not deny it, but it is in what capacity he was signing that matters.

Mr MacBride: You mentioned the words 'statutory agent'.

Mr de Valera: You are playing with words.

Mr MacBride: I will leave that to the people. They will be well able to judge that.[10]

The republic was proclaimed on the anniversary of the 1916 Rising, Easter Monday 1949. Maud Gonne MacBride was one of those who attended the solemn High Mass and Te Deum in Dublin's Pro Cathedral. Harry S. Truman, the US President, sent a message of congratulations, as did King George V, the Commonwealth Dominions, the Pope, and many other world leaders. The occasion in Ireland was a strangely muted one, caused in part by Fianna Fáil's anger at being upstaged.

Noel Browne has written of these events in his dispassionate style, saying:

The process of the repeal of the External Relations Act was irresponsible, incredible and ludicrous.... It was surely both ill-mannered and ungracious of Fine Gael and Mr. Costello to deprive Seán MacBride of his rights, as the relevant Minister, to introduce the Bill repealing the External Relations Act. Mr. Costello chose to introduce the Bill himself. MacBride, in a pitiful protest, did not appear at the Easter Sunday march-past and volleys from the roof of the G.P.O. In his absence, I acted as Minister for External Affairs at the circus.[11]

Speaking in the Dáil in May, MacBride said:

All these indications of the Government's policy and intention were given before the Taoiseach's press conference in Ottawa on 7 September 1948, in the course of which, confirming the reports which had already appeared in the press, he stated that the External Relations Act, being full of inaccuracies and infirmities, the Irish Government were preparing to repeal it.[12]

Ireland left the Commonwealth, but Irish citizens lost no rights in Britain and normal trade continued with that country. John Costello explained in the Dáil: 'The result of all these questions and discussions which took place was that both the Minister [MacBride] and myself, came down on the line that we were not members of the Commonwealth.'[13]

Ireland and Britain retained a very special relationship, though Britain responded with its Ireland Act 1949. This recognised that 'Eire ceased to be part of His Majesty's Dominions'. It also 'declared that Northern Ireland ... in no event will cease to be part of His Majesty's Dominions and of the United Kingdom without the consent of the Parliament of Northern Ireland'. Thus Partition was strengthened further.

As Minister for External Relations, MacBride was attending many international gatherings and usually spoke about the injustice of Partition. He constantly brought up Partition at the Council of Europe and at the OEEC. The American State Department kept firmly to the view that Partition was a matter for the Irish and British governments and the US should not get involved. Dean Acheson, the American Secretary of State, was fearful that a conflict in Ireland over Partition would endanger the Allies' post-war security network. The USA was anxious that Ireland should join NATO, the new defence association that was about to be set up. But, despite meetings with Acheson and Harry Truman, MacBride could not persuade the Americans to see Ireland other than through a British perspective. All MacBride could tell the Dáil was that: 'President Truman expressed, in no uncertain terms, the friendship of his Government and of the people of the U.S.A. for Ireland and his desire for the closest link possible between the two countries.'[14]

When the invitation to join NATO came to MacBride, he replied saying: 'In these circumstances, any military alliance with ... the State that is responsible for the unnatural division of Ireland, which occupies a portion of our country with its armed forces, and which supports undemocratic institutions in the north-eastern corner of Ireland, would be entirely repugnant and unacceptable to the Irish people. No Irish Government, whatever its political views, could participate with Britain in a military alliance, while this situation continues, without running counter to the national sentiment of the Irish people.'[15]

Terence Brown has written that 'these two acts of foreign policy [the declaration of the Republic, and NATO] ... meant that de Valera's long-term republican policy was prosecuted with a directness and haste he would not have wished.... Sean MacBride was in all probability the man who pressed the issue.'[16]

MacBride persuaded the government to pass an Irish News Agency Act 1949 on 21 December 1949, empowering the Minister for External Affairs to promote a company that would publish news information. Up to that, most news came from British sources, to an international audience. In the Dáil he explained: 'As a result of the development of national newspapers and of news agencies, gradually public opinion came to be more influential in relation to foreign policy.... Now the supply of accurate and objective information concerning news and developments in other countries, has come to be an essential part of the democratic process.... We have no independent Irish News Agency.... We have to counteract a good deal of hostile propaganda about Ireland that is published constantly in the Press of the world.'[17]

16

European Statesman

An Anti-Partition League flourished in 1949 among all the political parties and received support from the Irish throughout the world. It ran political campaigns in the North and in Britain. In time, it indirectly led to a renewal of an IRA campaign in the North. Brian Faulkner in *Memoirs of a Statesman* [1978] writes of the period:

> The Election of 1949 was fought almost totally on Ulster's place within the U.K. That this should be so, was determined by a particularly ill judged and offensive piece of interference from the Dublin Government. In 1949 Eire had decided to leave the British Commonwealth and declare a Republic (an action which drove even further wedges between Irishmen, North and South). Sean MacBride, a former I.R.A. leader then Minister for External Affairs, was helping to stir up the Nationalists inside Ulster and an all-party anti-Partition Fund was set up. The Election in Northern Ireland became notorious as the 'Chapel Gate Election' due to the decision of the Fund's organisers to hold collections outside all Roman Catholic Chapels in Ireland on the Sunday before polling day.[1]

Despite Faulkner's harsh words, MacBride had a cordial meeting with Sir Basil Brooke, Prime Minister of Northern Ireland at this time, though nothing materialised from it. Mr W. Topping, the Unionist Chief Whip, also attended and made several trips to Dublin subsequently to see MacBride.

An American diplomat wrote of MacBride's role at the OEEC: 'Ireland has participated in the Paris meetings of the

O.E.E.C. wherein MacBride's special abilities and temperament have filled him to perform useful services among the more important nations as a "leg-man", who had no special interest in European power politics. This ability conforms to the Irish contention that it is a nation with a long tradition of resistance to religious and political oppression and therefore in a position to find friends among other nations. The recent establishment of diplomatic relations with India is symptomatic.'[2]

MacBride was Vice-President of the OEEC from 1948 to 1951 and for the first two of those years was President of the Committee of Ministers of the Council. In this period, he was a sponsor and signatory of four major international accords: the Convention for European Economic Co-operation (Paris, 1948), the Statute of the Council of Europe (London, 1949), the Geneva Convention for the Protection of War Victims (1949), and the European Convention of Human Rights (Rome, 1950). These have proved to be some of the most important European Conventions ever passed. MacBride's intimate knowledge of them was to prove a huge benefit to him and to his work internationally later in his career.

Speaking on the approval of the Statute of the Council of Europe on 12 July 1949 in Dáil Eireann, MacBride took the occasion to consider some major developments within Europe. He regretted that currently they were only talking of an agreement between ten European nations. He admitted that the statute was a compromise between loose governmental contact and 'a closely-knit federation of States akin to the United States of America'. It was clear that he would have favoured the latter development, 'but at least it is a beginning which is capable of enlargement'. He said that 'ever since the break-up of the Roman Empire, the conception of European unity has continued to haunt the minds of philosophers and statesmen'. He named some of those, the Duc de Sully, chief adviser to Henry IV of France, the Abbe de Sainte Pierre, who wrote *Perpetual Peace*, the philosophers Bentham, Kant and Rousseau who termed his concept 'Utopian'. He said though that it was only in the nineteenth century that 'the process of regional federation in Europe made considerable progress in Germany, Switzerland and Italy'.

He instanced the Pan Europa movement founded in 1922 by Count Coudenhove-Kalergi as 'the first concrete step in the present century. Its first congress at Vienna in 1926 was attended by 'delegates from 23 European countries — many of them public men of high standing and authority'. In 1929 Aristide Briand, twelve times premier of France and a Nobel Peace Prize winner, raised the question of European unity officially at the Assembly of the League of Nations, where it was well received. But most countries were unwilling to accept any limitation whatever of sovereign rights. 'The Japanese conquest of Manchuria, the economic depression, the rise of Hitlerism, the Italian invasion of Abyssina and the civil war in Spain gradually diverted the minds of European Governments into other channels, and the idea of European unity was quietly dropped from the international agenda'.

After the war Winston Churchill became a firm advocate of European unity. In 1947 a Joint International Committee was formed which organised the Congress of Europe at The Hague in May 1948. This was succeeded by the European Movement with 'Messrs. Spaak, Churchill, de Gaspari and Leon Blum' as its Presidents. The resolutions of The Hague Congress were approved by the French Assembly in August 1948. A Joint International Committee drew up proposals suggesting that there should be a European assembly which would be purely advisory in character. The Brussels Treaty Consultative Group of five countries, not including Ireland, discussed the idea and announced in February 1949 that a conference would be held at which other European countries would be invited to be represented. Ireland received an invitation from Britain to attend a conference of Foreign Ministers on 3 May. A draft statute was approved. It was also agreed that the Consultative Assembly should meet in Strasbourg on the following 11 August, subsequent to a meeting of the Committee of Ministers.

MacBride then told the Dáil what he hoped the Council of Europe would achieve. He assured the deputies that the statute would not interfere with national independence or sovereignty. Though Europe was a 'main-spring of civilisation and culture which now spans the world, she has also been the storm centre and the origin of the wars...'. He said that the development of the atom bombs made another war 'frightening to contemplate'. New weapons will make 'the mass air-raids, the atom bombs and the extermination camps of the last war pale into insignificance, should another war take place. World War I, in effect, created a situation in central Europe which caused World War II ... it may sound Utopian and unrealistic to think that it is possible to avoid wars'. He then said that all that could be done to avoid future wars had to be done, to avoid a world-wide catastrophe. 'In the first part of the preamble — for which we, incidentally, were largely responsible — it is recognised that the pursuit of peace is vital to the preservation of human society and civilisation ... if we are to survive.' The new statute provided machinery for contact between European states, at Governmental level and at Parliamentary or representative levels.... It can create a public opinion, an ethical and moral basis which must govern human action and relationships. Two bodies were provided for, one a Committee of Foreign Ministers and the other a Consultative Assembly. The Committee of Foreign Ministers would wield whatever power the statute would confer. There would be eighty seven delegates to the Council of Europe from the ten-member countries, proportionate to population of France, Britain, Italy, Sweden, the Netherlands, Belgium, Ireland, Norway, Denmark and Luxembourg. Ireland would have four delegates to Britain's eighteen.

MacBride concluded:

> ... it is, in my view, one of the most important and constructive developments that have taken place in Europe. I hope it will evolve rapidly into a more closely-knit body that may lead to a Federated States of Europe ... it excludes from its ambit all questions of military measures. Unlike many other attempts at world organisations, it relies rather on moral, ethical, social and economic forces than upon military measures. I have pleasure in asking the House to ratify the statute.[3]

In his book, *West Briton*, Brian Inglis gives a version of the first full meeting of the Council of Europe at Strasbourg in 1950. It was Ireland's turn to take the chair and that honour fell to Seán MacBride. Inglis had been asked by Conor Cruise O'Brien, who had the responsibility for supervising the recently established Irish News Agency, to cover the meeting for the Agency. Inglis wrote of MacBride's address, which was delivered in French, as 'irritating the English delegates who thought he was being pretentious or offensive, and puzzling the French, who found his treatment of their language stilted. And in a carelessly supercilious phrase MacBride allowed himself to give the impression that the Ministers regarded themselves as wise parents controlling the childish whims of their unruly children — the Assembly delegates'.[4]

Inglis goes on to say that when the defence debate took place, the Irish delegates, including Eamon de Valera, William Norton and Seán MacEntee, deplored the fact that Ireland was unable to participate in European defence while it was partitioned and part of it occupied by another member state of the Council of Europe. According to Inglis, these contributions were received very badly by the assembled delegates, but the Irish felt obliged to use the occasion to make their point. The report of proceedings issued by the Irish News Agency and carried on its front page by *The Irish Times* made it clear that the comments of the Irish delegates had been met with hostility. This led to the Agency itself being treated in a hostile fashion by all the Irish delegates. Inglis writes that MacBride had already been disillusioned by the Agency's failure to meet the Irish delegation on its arrival in Strasbourg.[5]

The European Convention on Human Rights was one of the achievements Seán MacBride was most pleased with. It came to be a benchmark in the field of human rights. It has been used by Irish citizens acting as individuals against their own government and against British governments. It has been used by Irish governments against British governments. Many European governments have also used it. The main provisions within it on human rights are:

> Article 2.(1) Everyone's right to life shall be protected by law. No one shall be deprived of his life intentionally save in the execution of a sentence of a court following his conviction of a crime for which this penalty is provided by law ...

Article 3. No one shall be subjected to torture or to inhuman or degrading treatment or punishment.

Article 4.(1) No one shall be held in slavery or servitude.

(2) No one shall be required to perform forced or compulsory labour.

Article 5.(1) Everyone has the right to liberty and security of person.

Article 8.(1) Everyone has the right to respect for his private and family life, his home and his correspondence ...

Article 9.(1) Everyone has the right to freedom of thought, conscience and religion ...

Article 10.(1) Everyone has the right to freedom of expression ...

Dealing with the estimates vote for his department on 13 July 1949 MacBride spoke on a wide number of matters. He first of all called for a non-party approach on external affairs policy, offering all information available to the Leader of the Opposition. He paid tribute to his departmental staff for their 'self-sacrificing enthusiasm'. Because of a shortage of staff, he expressed thanks 'that the Russian veto on our admission to the United Nations Organisation has been maintained'. He reported that since 18 April official recognition was accorded to the Republic of Ireland internationally. India, Norway and Egypt proposed to open embassies in Dublin.

MacBride defended 'the Government decision declining to adhere to the Atlantic Pact' (NATO), because of the implication involved of accepting the border. He said that it was outside interference in the affairs of other countries, which caused the last war. He said 'the fact that Britain succeeded, over 25 years ago, in retaining a corner of our island ... in no way entitled her to divide the historic Irish nation and to pretend that our island now consists of two separate nations'. He claimed that in an area approximating four of the six counties ... there is a majority in favour of unity: 'the nationalist population in these areas is coerced ... to remain separated from the rest of Ireland'. He then spoke of the unionists: 'we are quite prepared to afford them any constitutional guarantees that might be reasonably required to allay any fears … we cannot, however, 'accept the claim of a small minority supported by Britain to divide our nation'.

The Minister held that partition was essentially undemocratic and he regretted that the American State Department policy precluded any American assistance in 'bringing about a discussion and an ultimate solution of this question'. He adverted to the suggestion 'that the USA have, under the provisions of the Atlantic Charter, undertaken to defend Britain's invasion of our territorial integrity'. He added that Ireland had to get its view on partition across worldwide. This cost money and his department was short staffed. He hoped that the Irish News Agency would assist, but felt that Irish embassies abroad should contribute. He noted 'when I came into the department … we had not as much as one press attache, one information officer or one public relations officer abroad'. He had initiated the setting up of an information section within the department. He proposed enlarging diplomatic staff across America and in London.

He then mentioned in some detail an Advisory Committee on Cultural Relations with other countries that he had set up earlier. He thanked its chairman, Mr Justice Gavan Duffy (the same man who had been the last signatory to the Treaty and before whom MacBride had argued many legal cases). He outlined some of the committee's activities: reproducing twenty copies of the Book of Kells, granting £250 to the Gaelic League of London, granting £300 to a review on Celtic Studies published in Paris, publishing a pamphlet on theatre by Micheal MacLiammoir, grant-aiding participation in the International Folk Music Festival in Venice, making a grant to the Royal Society of Antiquaries.

MacBride then turned his attention to the dangers of religious persecution abroad. He spoke of 'what appears to be a concerted attack on religion generally in the Communist-dominated States of Central Europe … the Catholic Church has been the principal victim of this persecution'. He said that a representative of the Irish government had sought access to the imprisoned Cardinal Mindszenty in Hungary, but was refused. He went on: 'in voicing our abhorrence of this religious persecution, I am expressing the views of every member of the House. In addition to the fact that we are a predominantly Catholic nation, our whole history has been one of struggle for the achievement of civil and religious liberty'. He then spoke of so many Irish missionaries operating in the Far East, China, Korea, Hong Kong, Burma, Malaya. He said that the spread of communism there, put not only the work of the Irish missionaries in peril, but their own personal safety too. He announced that he was seeking to appoint consular representatives in some of those countries.

MacBride continued on a religious theme, speaking next about the protection of the Holy Places in Palestine. These 'should be suitably protected and free access ensured for all religions ... the whole area of Jerusalem should be placed under international control'. He noted that the United Nations was addressing the matter. He said 'before the Government accorded de facto recognition to the State of Israel on 1 February', he sought and received assurances that 'Israel would agree to putting the Holy Places under an international regime'.

The Minister reported on how his department was promoting Irish exports. He mentioned trade agreements with Britain, France, the Netherlands and trade discussions with Sweden, Italy, Spain, Belgium and Western Germany. He told the Dáil that additional work would be required for the European Recovery Programme, from his already overstretched department. He said that Ireland's principal contribution to the Organisation for European Economic Recovery's programme would be in the field of agriculture.

On MacBride's conclusion, the leader of the opposition, Mr de Valera contributed. The bitterness between these two was always palpable, though each tried to avoid outright hostility in the Dáil chamber. He acknowledged that the department was understaffed. He said 'I congratulated the Minister last year on having escaped the axe which was threatened by the Minister for Finance, but I am half inclined to think now, that he has escaped even the pruning knife'. But Mr de Valera still intended to vote against the Estimates, because he 'cannot see definitely how the expenditure is to be of real value'.[6]

Seán Cronin quotes a CIA opinion of Seán MacBride in his

study of Washington's Irish policy: 'Like Costello, a brilliant and successful barrister, he is noted for his forceful advocacy and remarkable talent for cross-examination. He is probably the best debater in the Dáil. He is definitely of Prime Ministerial calibre. He is charming, affable and intelligent, an excellent diplomat.'[7]

17

Mother and Child Controversy

The coalition government was about to be torn asunder in a debacle, which has secured it a permanent place in the folklore of Irish political life, the Mother and Child controversy.

Public health policy in Ireland was alarmingly ineffective. Malnutrition, infant mortality and tuberculosis were taking a terrible toll. In 1946 Fianna Fáil published a Bill to improve the general health services. It dealt with infectious diseases, school medical services, free medical care for mothers and children, without a means test. Medical consultants saw a danger to their monetary awards in the scheme, if a state service became operative. The Catholic Bishops objected privately that 'for the State to empower the Public Authority to provide for the health of all children, and to treat their ailments, and to educate women in regard to health, and to provide them with gynaecological services, was directly and entirely contrary to Catholic Social teaching, the rights of the family, the rights of the Church in Education, and the rights of the Medical profession and other voluntary institutions.'[1]

The new coalition government inherited the Health Act and Noel Browne became the Minister for Health on his first day in the Dáil. He was totally committed to his brief and achieved great success in the fight against TB. Browne was lucky in that MacBride had already cleared the way for him by getting agreement on the necessary finance via the Hospitals Sweepstakes. Spending on hospital building went from £2 million in 1947 to £3 million in 1951. The number of hospital beds increased from 2,000 to 8,000. Inoculation, radiography and a national blood transfusion scheme were initiated. Noel Browne was not hamstrung by the Department of Finance, and he became a crusader for the eradication of tuberculosis. Several of his family had died from the disease and in 1950 Browne announced that he would bring into force free post and antenatal care for mothers, and free services for the children, all without a means test. The medical consultants were worried, but they knew the bishops were on their side in their opposition to Browne's proposals. A key figure on the bishop's side was Dr John McQuaide, the Archbishop of Dublin, a doctor's son. Noel Browne did not get cabinet approval for the details of his scheme before declaring his intention to proceed. He also thought, quite mistakenly, that he had satisfied a delegation of the bishops, when he met them in October. This was a grave error as the Secretary to the Hierarchy wrote shortly afterwards to the Taoiseach, stating their firm objections:

Dear Taoiseach:

The Archbishops and Bishops of Ireland, at their meeting on October 19th, had under consideration the proposal for Mother and Child health service and other kindred medical services. They recognize that these proposals are motivated by a sincere desire to improve public health but they feel bound by their office to consider whether the proposals are in accordance with Catholic moral teaching.

In their opinion, the powers taken by the State in the proposed Mother and Child health service are in direct opposition to the rights of the family and of the individual and are liable to very great abuse. Their character is such that no assurance that they would be used in moderation could justify their enactment. If adopted in law they would constitute a ready-made instrument for future totalitarian aggression....

The Bishops desire that your Government should give careful consideration to the dangers inherent in the present proposals before they are adopted by the Government for legislative enactment, and, therefore, they feel it their duty to submit their views on this subject to you privately and at the earliest opportunity, since they regard the issues involved as of the greatest moral and religious importance.

I remain, dear Taoiseach,
Yours very sincerely,
/s/ JAMES STAUNTON
Bishop of Ferns,
Secretary to the Hierarchy.

John A. Costello, TD, Taoiseach.

Noel Hartnett was a very close friend of Noel Browne. He had brought Browne into Clann na Poblachta and had introduced him to MacBride. As relations between Hartnett and MacBride deteriorated, so did MacBride sense a certain hostility from Browne. In November 1950, at a dinner in the Russell Hotel, Browne told MacBride (according to MacBride) that his leadership of the party was abysmal and that he, Browne, intended to break up the Clann and the government. Browne denies making such threats, but from then on, MacBride felt that Browne was waiting for an opportunity to act against himself and the party.

In his last interview for television recorded before his death in 1988, but not broadcast until January 1992, MacBride spoke of this meeting. He said:

> There was a lull in the Dáil; we could leave the Dáil for a couple of hours. I took him to dinner with me in the Russell Hotel and then he unfolded to me what was his view of things, that he thought I was a hopeless leader; that Clann na Poblachta was useless; that the InterParty Government was no good and that he was going to try to bring it down; and bring down Clann unless he could control it…. And this came to me as a complete bombshell of surprise at the time. I made a full note of that interview and gave it to the Chairman of our Executive, Donal O'Donoghue, because I felt that once you're involved personally in a thing, once you're under attack yourself, it's much better for someone else to handle it. Donal tried to handle it: had several interviews with Browne and all that, but with no success.[2]

Louie O'Brien confirms that as soon as MacBride returned to Iveagh House from the Russell Hotel, she typed up his memorandum of the conversation with Noel Browne.[3] MacBride

produced this memorandum on several occasions over the
years to prove his version of what had taken place.

Noel Browne wrote of this meeting too and claimed that he
said if Clann na Poblachta and the government gave in to the
demands of the Catholic Church, such a move would seriously
undermine a united Ireland. He wrote, 'I warned him that I
intended to publicise to the full any such interference by the
Church, should it occur, in Cabinet affairs'.[4]

On 22 February 1951 *The Irish Times* reported that a division existed in Clann na Poblachta. Some members, like Dr
Browne and Noel Hartnett, felt that the party was in danger
of losing its radical soul; others believed that the party was
serving the country best by staying in government.

The Minister for Posts and Telegraphs, James Everett,
appointed a political associate as postmaster of Baltinglass,
County Wicklow, overlooking a good local candidate. It caused
a national furore. Noel Browne and Noel Hartnett felt that
Clann na Poblachta should leave the government on the
issue. MacBride disagreed feeling that the issue did not merit
such action. Browne resigned from the standing committee
of the party; Hartnett resigned from the party in February
1951. Noel Hartnett had been a most vital part of the success
of the Clann from the beginning. He had failed to win a Dáil
seat in the 1948 general election and had not been put forward
for nomination to the Senate by MacBride. As time went on,
he became embittered with MacBride. As a government
minister and as chief of staff of the IRA, MacBride had not the
facility or will to win friends and influence those whose
support was vital for him.

MacBride was out of the country for most of March 1951.
On his return he discovered that the row between Browne and
the Catholic bishops was unresolved and was about to become
public. MacBride called a meeting of the Ard Comhairle and
Comhairle Seasmhach of Clann na Poblachta, to ensure that
he would have party support in the turbulent days ahead. As
the later document published by Clann shows, MacBride
had the party solidly behind him, even if it came to dismissing
Browne from government.

In March 1951 Browne declared that he intended to go
ahead with the scheme, again without explicit cabinet

approval. Costello wrote to Browne on 21 March saying, 'My withholding of approval of the scheme is due to the objections set forth in the letter to me from the Secretary to the Hierarchy, written on behalf of the Hierarchy, and to the reiteration of their objections by his Grace the Archbishop of Dublin, as Archbishop of Dublin'.

This controversy was provoking a debate that was embarrassing the government. Noel Browne wanted to compromise and believed that he had a way out, by offering to let the bishops pronounce on the Catholic morality of his scheme. He agreed to accept their ruling. But the bishops outmanoeuvred him and denounced the scheme as merely conflicting with Catholic social teaching.

When Costello told Browne formally, that the Health Scheme could not go ahead as envisaged, due to the objections of the bishops, a cabinet meeting was called. At that meeting Browne asked each minister whether he would support the Health Scheme, as things stood. Each of them refused, including MacBride. Browne then left the meeting, asking for time to consider his position. Then the Irish Congress of Trades Unions became involved and went into consultation with Browne. He let it be known, publicly, that at the request of the ICTU, he was reconsidering his resignation. This was too much for his cabinet colleagues. They decided that the time had come for them to break with him as a government minister. In cabinet MacBride had said: 'It is of course impossible for us to ignore the views of the Hierarchy. Even if we as Catholics were prepared to take the responsibility of disregarding their views, which I do not think we can do, it would be politically impossible to do so. We must therefore accept the views of the Hierarchy in this matter.'

MacBride then wrote to Browne saying that he was forced by the situation, largely created by Browne, to seek his resignation.

MacBride's letter to Browne was probably the most crucial he ever wrote. I include most of it here. Browne's reply, despite its venom, covers many important points. It also refers to the wider problems between the two men.

Dear Dr Browne,

Following upon your own declarations and the indications given by me, I had hoped that it would not have been necessary to write this letter. Unfortunately, by reason of the situation which has arisen, and for which I fear you are largely responsible, I have no alternative, as leader of Clann na Poblachta, but to request you to transmit, as soon as possible, your resignation as Minister for Health to the Taoiseach.

You will no doubt realise that, in the light of the events that have happened, it would not now be possible for you to implement successfully the Mother and Child health service, which is urgently required and which both the Government and the Clann have undertaken to provide. The prolongation of the present situation can only further delay the provision of the service, and is, in my view, highly detrimental not merely to the Clann, but also to the national interest. The creation of a situation where it is made to appear that a conflict exists between the spiritual and temporal authorities is always undesirable; in the case of Ireland, it is highly damaging to the cause of national unity, and should have been avoided.

In my view, the creation of this situation and the long delays that have occurred in the provision of the service were as unnecessary as they were damaging to the national interest, to the Government, and to Clann na Poblachta.

As the leader of a new party which has taken a share in responsibility for the management of the country's affairs, I feel that I owe to the nation, to the Government, and to the Clann, the duty of ensuring that any Minister for whom I am responsible, discharges his duties with that high standard of conduct which is required in Government.

Lest it be sought to represent, as has been done studiously for some time past, in the Press and elsewhere, that my actions indicate in some respect opposition to Mother and Child health services, I wish to state categorically that the establishment, with the minimum delay, of such services in the freest sense of the word and with the least impediment possible, has been my earnest wish. My complaint is that situations are being created unnecessarily which can only cause delays and added difficulties....

I should like to assure you that, in reaching the decision that has compelled me to write this letter, I have sincerely sought to eliminate from my mind the other events, not connected with the Mother and Child services, which have rendered our collaboration increasingly difficult in the course of the last year. I can assure you that these events will not preclude me from extending to you my fullest co-operation in the future for the achievement of the tasks which Clann na Poblachta undertook if you are prepared to co-operate to this end.

Yours sincerely,
Sean MacBride

A copy of this letter is being sent to the Taoiseach for his information.

Dear Mr MacBride,

I received at a late hour last night your letter calling for my resignation. Your action did not surprise me, as it was in full conformity with the standards of behaviour which I have learned to expect from you. As I informed you on last Saturday, I proposed to resign on the following day (Sunday).

I explained at the executive meeting on Sunday and by a statement to the Press that I had deferred my action pending an outcome of the negotiations which had been initiated by the Trade Union Congress with a view to reaching a solution which would meet the views of the Hierarchy and still enable a non-means test scheme to be introduced. It was only for this reason that I deferred my resignation.

Your letter is a model of the two-faced hypocrisy and humbug so characteristic of you. Your references to a conflict between the spiritual and temporal authorities will occasion a smile among the many people who remember the earlier version of your kaleidoscopic self.

On the other side is your envenomed attack on me at the executive meeting last Sunday because, among other charges of my political inexperience, I had allowed myself to be photographed with the Protestant Archbishop of Dublin. This puerile bigotry is scarcely calculated to assist the cause of national reunification which you profess to have at heart.

Your references to my immaturity are surely gratuitous. My experience of democratic politics began only a few weeks subsequent to your own. I did not, however, have much to unlearn.

I have had a bitter experience of your cruel and authoritarian mind. It is my fervent hope that the destiny of this country will never be fully placed in your hands, because it would, in my view, mean the destruction of all those ideals which are part and parcel of Christian democracy.

Again, may I comment on your reference to 'that high standard of conduct which is required in government'. Inside the Cabinet and outside in conversations with you I have protested against the making of appointments on a corrupt basis and against other irregularities. May I instance as one example the reasons for my resignation from the Standing Committee. Your defence when these matters were raised at our party executive meeting by a former member was that 'unsavoury matters are inseparable from politics'. This view I cannot accept.

I entered politics because I believed in the high-minded principles which you were expounding on political platforms. I do you no injustice when I state that I have never observed you hearken to any of these principles when practical cases came before us. I have tried to analyse your curious philosophy not very successfully. Expediency is your sole yardstick, and to expediency you are prepared to subordinate all principles sacred and profane.

I have today sent to the general secretary my resignation from the Clann na Poblachta Party. I have bidden farewell to your unwholesome brand of politics. Despite my experiences at your hand, I am not so cynical as to believe that you typify the ordinary politically conscious person in this country. May God forbid that you should.

I am, as demanded by you, today sending my resignation to the Taoiseach.

Yours faithfully,
Noel C. Browne

Noel Browne released much of the correspondence between himself and the various parties involved with the introduction of the Mother and Child health scheme to the Press. This proved sensational because such correspondence was normally kept out of the public domain. It placed enormous pressure on MacBride and Costello, who were called upon to defend their positions in public. Browne was cast as the knight in shining armour, thwarted by his supposed allies. MacBride and Clann na Poblachta were most vulnerable to Browne's revelations. MacBride responded by releasing a devastating statement from the Clann, which sought to show that the party had given Browne every chance to behave responsibly, but whose behaviour left MacBride with no choice, but to sack him.[5]

As it is sought to represent that the events leading up to Dr. Browne's resignation from Clann na Poblachta, have their sole origin in the proposed Mother and Child Health Service, it has become necessary to release for publication the following resolution which was adopted unanimously by the Ard Comhairle at its meeting of March 31st — April 1st last: 'That the Ard Comhairle view with grave concern and disapproval the attitude and conduct of Dr. Browne and is perturbed by his lack of co-operation and by his apparent disloyalty to the leadership of the Party and require him to show a greater degree of loyalty and co-operation in his dealings with the leadership.

The Ard Comhairle reiterates its support for the Mother and Child Service but it considers it necessary however to express its fear that the successful implementation of this service may be jeopardised by the manner in which the whole problem is being handled by Dr. Browne....

That the Ard Comhairle wish to put on record that if the leader of the Party deems it necessary to call for the resignation or removal of Dr. Browne from the Government, he can rely on the loyal support of the Ard Comhairle. Dr. Browne's lack of candour, irresponsibility and disloyalty had been considered by the Coiste Seasmhach and the Ard Comhairle for some months ... and the foregoing resolutions were adopted only after the most careful consideration, in a final effort to avoid the position which he has now deliberately created. They were not published or circularised to the Organisation until all hope that Dr. Browne would behave responsibly had to be abandoned....'

MacBride's dismissal of the radical and popular Browne was a great political error. No doubt Browne was a difficult person, but he epitomised part of what Clann na Poblachta espoused, a searing social conscience, and he had won the admiration of many voters.

In the Dáil debate on Noel Browne's resignation, he himself said: 'I have been led to believe that my insistence on the exclusion of a means test had the full support of my colleagues in Government. I now know that it had not.... On the 9th of March I received a letter from His Grace the Archbishop of Dublin. From this letter I was surprised to learn that His Grace might not approve of the scheme.... I trust that the standards manifested in these dealings are not customary in the public life of this, or any other democratic nation....'.

Oliver Flanagan, a Fine Gael TD, asked for an 'opportunity to be given for the purpose of discussing the allegations made by Deputy Dr. Browne against the Minister for External Affairs for participating in corrupt practices'. Deputy Paddy Smith referred to Seán MacBride as 'Pontius Pilate'.

The Taoiseach, John Costello, said that, 'The Minister for External Affairs told me he felt that as he had been responsible for introducing Deputy Browne as a member of the Government and as he felt he had not fulfilled the trust he had reposed in him, it was his duty to ask him to resign.' Costello said that he was not in the least bit afraid of *The Irish Times* or any other newspaper. 'I as a Catholic,' he continued, 'obey my Church authorities and will continue to do so, in spite of *The Irish Times* or anything else ... the Hierarchy confine themselves strictly to faith and morals ... it was because the then Minister for Health took the unusual course of saying: "I want a special, authoritative decision from the Hierarchy in general meeting and an immediate decision," that this matter took the form it finally took. The fact that it is now a matter of public controversy is entirely due to the fact that he published all these documents, for his own purposes and his own motives, in the newspapers this morning.'

MacBride was the next speaker. He said he felt that he should be in a position at all times to assure the Taoiseach that the members of his Party in the government are worthy of the confidence of the government. He then read his letter to Costello, which included his own letter requesting Noel Browne's resignation and the reasons for such a request. He regretted that he had not acted earlier, but had not due to the high regard he had for Noel Browne's work. He said that the science of government involved the task of ensuring a harmonious relationship between Churches on the one hand and the civil government on the other...

> ... it is also regrettable that a position should ever arise in which the action of the Government, or the action of one of its Ministers, should become the subject of review or of criticism by the Hierarchy.... In many countries, political Parties are based on religious affiliations. That I conceive to be undesirable. We here in Ireland have avoided that division of Parties. There are no Catholics, Protestants and Jews in, I trust, this House, and political divisions have never been built upon religious faith.... Those of us in this House who are Catholics, and all of us in the Government who are Catholics are, as such of course, bound to give obedience to the rulings of our Church and of our Hierarchy.... In this case, we are dealing with the considered views of the leaders of the Catholic church to which the vast majority of our people belong. These views cannot be ignored and must be given full weight. In my considered view, having been fairly closely associated with the events that have taken place in recent months in connection with this whole matter, I am satisfied, beyond doubt, that the clash which has occurred was completely unnecessary and could have been avoided. It is a clash which is highly damaging to the national interest. I fear that little or no attempt was made by my late colleague to avoid the clash, and I am not even certain that he did not provoke it.

MacBride then spent some time dissecting Noel Browne's earlier speech. He noted that Browne claimed that he was left in ignorance of the views of the Hierarchy. MacBride said 'that cannot have been so, having regard to the facts as I know them.' He said that he had several discussions with Browne on the fears of the Hierarchy, and advised him to discuss the matter with members of the Hierarchy. MacBride said he was so anxious about the position that he had even mentioned it at a meeting of the executive of Clann na Poblachta in February and on numerous other occasions before witnesses. On 8 March before leaving for the USA he both spoke and wrote to Browne, saying:

> If an opportunity arises of securing even the tacit co-operation of the doctors, you should avail of it. Likewise as I told you, I think that the Hierarchy are by no means satisfied as to certain provisions of the scheme and that you should seek their co-operation. I am certain that, if properly approached, their opposition to the scheme could at least be minimised and, possibly, their approval secured for it.

MacBride said that the whole purport of Browne's Dáil statement was that he did not realise there were any objections from the Hierarchy. MacBride added that originally when the scheme came before the government, it came in the memorandum brought forward by Browne, which accompanied the heads of a bill to implement the Health Act of 1947. One of the amendments envisaged by the legislation was to authorise the making of charges for services performed. MacBride then said that 'Deputy Browne sought the approval of the Government, therefore, to introduce amending legislation so that this scheme could be charged for'. MacBride said that he could not see why working people should have to pay additional taxation to provide free medical services, 'for people earning more than £1,000 a year, for instance'. He then argued that 'on the basis of the principle, it would have been possible to reach agreement without infringing any of the doctrines of the Catholic Church ... I am quite satisfied that if Deputy Dr Browne had desired to evolve a scheme which conformed to the views expressed by the Hierarchy, such a scheme could have been evolved and would be at least partly in operation by now. The only time the matter came before the Government was in the month of June, 1948.'[6]

Shortly after this debacle, the inter-party government was forced to go to the country when three rural TDs ended their support for the government over the price of milk. Even at this stage the future of Clann na Poblachta was in grave doubt. Three of its TDs chose to sit as Independents and another joined the Labour Party. Clann na Poblachta nominated only twenty-six candidates in the election, a far cry from the hopes and expectations of 1948. Only MacBride and their Cavan candidate, John Tully, won seats.

It had been a most bitter election and the electorate was still in shock at the revelations of the goings on in government and the total capitulation to the Catholic hierarchy. In the event MacBride was lucky to hold his own seat. He received 2,853 first preference votes (he had received 8,648 in 1948) and was elected only on the eleventh count, without reaching the quota. In a rare display of hurt, MacBride wrote to Costello:

> The effect of the electorate's decision is a repudiation of the policies I have been advocating and of my action in the course of the last three years. That this decision was brought about by the treacherous or irresponsible actions of but a few people, does not alter the results which flow from the verdict of the people. That verdict would nullify the usefulness of any work I could do, as a member of the Government at home, and preclude me from speaking for the country abroad. In these circumstances, I do not consider that my services in the Government are of any particular value to the country and therefore, I feel entitled to be released from future duty in Government.

In his reply, Costello complimented MacBride on the discharge of his ministerial duties, 'exhausting yourself to the extent of often causing me anxiety for your health'. He said that it was due to MacBride's work, ability and personal qualities that Ireland had been able to take such a prominent and nationally beneficial part in the activities of the OEEC. He fully recognised what the Minister's efforts internationally had achieved towards the ending of partition and his success particularly in the United States, of securing much influential support for the cause of Irish unity.'

The full election result was Fianna Fáil 69, Fine Gael 40, Labour 16, Clann na Talmhan 6, Clann na Poblachta 2, and

Independents 14. Fine Gael did very well in the election, winning nine extra seats. Clann na Poblachta dropped from 13 per cent to 4 per cent of first preference votes. Noel Browne and two other Clann na Poblachta candidates who broke with MacBride, Peadar Cowan and Jack McQuillan, polled very well and were elected. De Valera was elected Taoiseach in a minority government.

On the nomination of Taoiseach, MacBride requested de Valera to form a national government. He said, 'I have respect for the Taoiseach. I have known him and worked with him; I have followed his leadership during the Civil War and before the Civil War; I have probably, from this side of the House, a greater degree of respect for his political attitude in the course of the last 30 years....'[7]

Seán MacBride cut a lonely figure in that Dáil and was continually attacked by Fianna Fáil. He replied in kind, particularly to de Valera and Seán MacEntee, who showed him nothing but ridicule and hostility.

MacBride bore the personal odium of liberals who saw the government's capitulation to the dictat of the Catholic bishops as another vindication that 'Home rule is Rome rule'. He also became the political scapegoat, while John A. Costello and other ministers remained almost unscathed. This vilification is best seen in a cruel caricature penned for *The Leader* in August 1952 by Jack B. Yeats. In it Yeats considers MacBride as a clown, à la Charlie Chaplain, and also as a Don Quixote who has broken with his Sancho Panza (Noel Hartnett). It says in part:

> When he laughs ... the remarkable eyes, prominent and yet recessed, like those of some mad monk of romance ... the bandit eyebrows giving a touch of diablerie ... you feel you have been exposed to the reaction of an unknown ray.
>
> In repose ... the face ... is as if one of those death masks, of Tone or Emmet ... were to open its eyes and look out at you.... These are the masks of Comedy and Tragedy.... Mr. MacBride like Charlie Chaplain looks wistfully at the world: he is full of unrequited loves: for the Six Counties, for journalists, for the Fianna Fáil party, for the constituency of Dublin South-West. He often pleads his case in the

Dáil.... Confronted with bulky grim realities, Charlie is often a sad figure. But there is also a dream world — in which he is a brilliantly successful statesman, elegant, eloquent, strolling with the leaders of Europe: what he is doing is not very clear, but with what distinction he does it.... The dream of course was not all a dream ... the politician who insists on being known as 'The Leader' ... this thin-lipped fanatic, whose very laughter is somewhat chilling ... that even an authoritarian Chaplain is not quite unimaginable, when one has seen 'The Great Dictator'.

The word is like a knell: at any rate it has been so for Mr. MacBride.... Most people around him were inclined to do what he told them, should the sky fall, which it did.... His main achievement ... was to get the Commonwealth Party to take Ireland out of the Commonwealth....

Mr. MacBride is much more like Jan Masaryk [the Czech foreign minister who died in mysterious circumstances in 1948] than he is like Nero or Hitler.... He thinks he is using people who are really using him. These were the gifts that led to the debacle, when he and his young rival ... rolled together into the political abyss.... What symbol for so complex a man?... Don Quixote.... The gaunt knight, wistful yet severe in the delapidated La Mancha of Roebuck, has been reading tales of chivalry.... He will rescue the fair lady Cathleen Ni Houlihan from the castle Discrimination, where the British giant, Gerrymandering, holds her in thrall. The ogre Sterling, bars the way with his famous Link which will have to be snapped. The good fairies from America will help to accomplish this.... He saddles his spavined mare, Poblaclante and gallops down the drive. But something is missing. He calls aloud for Sancho Panza. But Sancho will never come again. Sancho has locked himself into the lodge.[8]

Given the prevailing culture, MacBride acted honourably and reasonably during the Mother and Child Scheme episode. There is cause to suppose that the issue was fastened onto and used to destroy him and Clann na Poblachta. He knew what he was doing and the possible consequences, but was not adroit enough to be a successful party politician.

18

Opposition Deputy

Reading the *Dáil Debates* for the years 1951 to 1957, when MacBride was in opposition, there is the same unacceptance of him as when he was the chief of staff of the IRA. Fianna Fáil felt great animosity towards him for interrupting their single party government. Fianna Fáil was representative of a cute peasant mentality in Irish society, which will fling all the mud available against an opponent. There was plenty of that around MacBride. There were also personality clashes which MacBride was involved in with his own ex-party colleagues. Unfortunately for him, these men continued to be re-elected to the Dáil and so personal acrimony with these was never far away from the floor of the chamber, especially when MacBride no longer held ministerial office.

Although MacBride was an assiduous debater and meant well, he did grate on people because he appeared too smart. Despite his best intentions, he often acted as if he had all the answers. He had opinions on everything. He admitted that he admired de Valera, but Fianna Fáil was not a party to forgive the past. It believed that it was the purest of the pure, that it was the 'national party'. It would not coalesce or share power with any outsider, least it compromise itself and its grip on the national identity and future.

During the early months of the new Dáil, one former colleague of MacBride's, Captain Peadar Cowan, tried to extend the hand of peace: 'In fact the one thing that I have taken a very strong pledge to do since we reassembled, is to endeavour to avoid being in conflict with Deputy MacBride. I ask Deputy MacBride to respond in that Christian spirit.'

This intervention occurred when MacBride was moving a motion 'that Dáil Eireann is of the opinion that a Select Committee of the House should be appointed to examine and report to the Dáil on the question of the desirability of the abolition of capital punishment.... I hope this can be considered away from any atmosphere of Party controversy.... The House will remember that up to 120 years ago a person could be executed for stealing 5 shillings or over. I think that very few people who commit serious crime, ever, in advance, consider the consequences of the crime.... My own view is that I would do away with Capital Punishment.'

MacBride made two interventions about the new British monarch, Elizabeth II, concerning her title and a Coronation party. He asked the Minister for External Affairs 'whether his attention had been drawn to the fact that in recordings broadcast by the BBC of the reading of the Proclamation of Accession of the new British Sovereign, she was described as Queen of Great Britain and Ireland.' He asked the Taoiseach 'If he and other members of the Government had received an invitation to attend a garden party to celebrate the coronation of the new British Queen: and if in view of the claim of sovereignty over a portion of Ireland made by the British Crown, he and other members of the Government propose to attend this celebration.'

One curious interplay between Eamon de Valera and MacBride showed the former in a very strange light, giving credence to those who believed that de Valera was a basically insecure person, resulting from his rejection by his mother. Concerning an incident in the Dáil restaurant where a Fianna Fáil deputy assaulted an opponent who had slighted him in the chamber, MacBride asked the Taoiseach: 'Does the Taoiseach propose to justify an effort at physical violence on every occasion in which there are verbal exchanges?' The Taoiseach replied 'If a person insults me and I have no redress other than to knock him down, and if I am fit to knock him down, I will do so....' MacBride later asked 'I take it the Taoiseach will reflect meanwhile on the statement he has just made.' The Taoiseach responded, 'I have reflected.'

MacBride spoke at length in debates on external affairs and economic affairs, particularly forestry. In late 1951 he took great glee in asking a question about one of his old enemies, the Central Bank: 'Has the Minister taken any steps to inform the OEEC that the Report of the Central Bank has been thrown overboard by the Government and by other parties in this House?'

MacBride was also conscious of the efforts being made by the Ulster Unionists to disparage the progress of the Republic. He asked: 'Has the Minister's attention been drawn to a propaganda card issued by the Ulster Unionist Council Belfast, and widely distributed throughout the world, alleging that the infantile death rate is 83/1000 in the twenty-six counties and 40/1000 in the six counties?'

On 27 July 1951, he asked the Minister for Education, Seán Moylan 'if he will make available to all national schools suitably framed copies of the Proclamation of 1916, and request that these be displayed in all the classrooms'. He further asked, 'Is the Minister prepared to consider the desirability of flying the National flag during school hours, from a pole provided for the purpose in each national school and to urge the formal hoisting and lowering of the flag daily in the presence of all the children and teachers'. He also asked the same minister 'whether he will urge primary and secondary schools to give instruction to children in the importance of afforestation and the care and protection of trees. Would the Minister consider the issuing of a circular to schools in relation to the organisation and holding of Arbor Week celebrations.' (In 1966, copies of the 1916 Proclamation were indeed distributed to all schools. In 1991 an Arbor Week for schools was held.)

MacBride was a political thinker and he tried to put new ideas before the Dáil. On a vote of confidence in the government in 1953 he said '… In 1951, I urged a national government.… I think we adopted too readily both the political and economic institutions of the country that had occupied us for centuries … unfortunately men like Griffith, Connolly, Pearse, Clarke, all the older and wiser men who had been the brains and inspiration of the Movement, ceased to be with us … we were left to carry on alone … best type of government … on the lines of the Swiss form, where most parties have representation in government.… We followed willy-nilly the policy laid down by the British Treasury.'[1]

Maud Gonne MacBride had never been afraid of death. She passed that on to her son, as she had got it from her father. As she reached her eighties, she sometimes longed for death. One of the people who became a very good friend to her in later life was Micheal MacLiammoir; she once told him that old age was hell. They both shared an interest in beauty and admired stylishness. Right to the end, she remained a fanatical hater of England and supported her son in all his political ventures. Francis MacManus, a Radio Eireann producer, got her to do a series of broadcast talks in 1949 on her long life. He wrote of her: 'Her age had its beauty. Her hair, fine as silk and still glossy, was whorled over her ears in an antique way.... There was witchcraft in her voice.... When she finished ... she smoked a cigarette and talked in quieter tones.'[2]

Most of her contemporaries were long since dead when she died in April 1953 at the age of eighty-six. Her family were with her as she received the last sacraments of the Church. She asked Iseult to give her the booties from her handbag, which went everywhere with her. They had belonged to her first-born child, George, who had died tragically as a baby. Then, looking radiant, she passed away.

Maud's death did not lead to major changes in Roebuck because she had been bedridden for a long time. Kid had been the matriarch of the household for a considerable period. On the day of Maud MacBride's burial in the republican plot in Glasnevin cemetery, an anonymous article in *The Irish Times* was rather mildly critical of her. It said she 'could or would talk about nothing except the manifold sins and wickedness of the British in Ireland.... There was a touch of magic about her, which persisted into the sourness of old age'. Kid responded immediately to this article and sent a letter to the Editor of *The Irish Times* which says as much about Kid herself as it does about her mother-in-law. It read in part:

> I have lived twenty-six years with Madame, and sourness and frustration are two things I should never have remotely connected with her. Sourness is for people who have not achieved, or who lack appreciation for, their achievements and are small enough to mind, but in Madame's case there

was plenty of appreciation from the people about whom she cared. All over the country there are people who bless her name. Frustration is for little people.... Nothing ever stopped Madame once set on a course, as various Governments and people have found out from time to time.

19

Supporting the Coalition

The government introduced an austerity programme which caused its downfall in May 1954, when some Independents failed to support it. The results of the election were : Fianna Fáil 65, Fine Gael 50, Labour 19, Clann na Talmhan 5, Clann na Poblachta 3, Others 5. Clann na Poblachta lost votes, but gained a seat. Fine Gael was the main beneficiary of the election. MacBride's personal vote had improved enormously from the 1951 debacle. He polled 6,151 first preference votes, compared to 2,853, and was elected on the ninth count at 8,475, after getting a large transfer from a Labour candidate. At first MacBride suggested a national government with John A. Costello as Taoiseach. He said: 'I feel certain that the President and His Eminence, Cardinal d'Alton, would willingly assist in the reconciliation of conflicting views. To dispel any ungenerous criticism that may be made of this initiative, let me state, as I did in 1951, that by reason of the small representation of my Party in the Dáil, I would not expect representation in such a national government.'[1]

In the event, Costello became Taoiseach of a coalition government with Labour and Clann na Talmhan. MacBride was offered a cabinet post, but the national executive of Clann na Poblachta forbade its members to participate in government, though it offered its support from without. MacBride replied to Costello's invitation declining with regret the invitation to join the inter-party government. He had no difference with the government's proposed policy and there was no disagreement on any particular ministry that he would occupy. He was wholeheartedly in favour of representative government, but it was to be regretted that his proposals for an all-party government did not evoke adequate acceptance. With only three seats in the Dáil, he said, Clann na Poblachta was not entitled to representation in government and the acceptance of a post would be invidious: 'With all the goodwill in the world, on the part of all concerned, I would ultimately find myself in the position of a lodger who was not paying for his keep.'2

On the nomination of the Taoiseach, MacBride said: '... the people have opted for an inter-party government.... Many of us are growing old. Many of the members of this House who are here today will probably not be in the next Dáil.... He [Costello] is a man of integrity, honour and ability.'3

The IRA had kept a reasonably low profile during the first inter-party government. An interesting development in the 1950s was a splinter party called Fianna Uladh, set up by Liam Kelly of Pomeroy, County Tyrone. He was expelled by the IRA for unauthorised military activity and set up his own party, which recognised the legitimacy of the Dáil. Kelly was elected to Stormont in 1953, but was immediately arrested and jailed. MacBride asked in the Dáil: 'I wonder could the Taoiseach say, as far as he is aware, whether there is any elected representative of the people in prison in any democratic country in Europe, outside the present case?'4

The anti-Partition League won seven seats in that same six-county election. When Kelly was released in 1954, Mac-Bride engineered a seat in Seanad Eireann for him, in an effort to woo the IRA away from abstentionist policies. Despite these efforts, Fianna Uladh soon disappeared and the IRA carried on as usual, planning a military campaign in the North. This involved carrying out cross-border attacks on military installations to get arms.

On a motion to grant an audience to all elected parliamentary representatives of the people, of the occupied counties, in the Dáil and Seanad, proposed by Deputy Jack McQuillan, MacBride said: '...Partition was imposed by Britain ... the people of the six counties have been and are continually denied their elementary democratic rights.... Listening both to the Leader of the Opposition and the Leader of the Government, it is quite clear neither has any policy in regarding the end of partition after thirty years ... we have no right to keep out the elected representatives of the people of the 6 counties.'[5]

MacBride continued to watch what the British had been doing when he asked the Minister for External Affairs whether his 'attention had been drawn to the summaries of the official records of the Yalta Conference, where Sir Winston Churchill had assured Marshal Stalin that he would be opposed to the admission of Ireland to membership of the United Nations.' In 1956 he also asked about British action in Cyprus: 'Is the Minister aware that the British Government notified the Council of Europe ... that they had deported persons from Cyprus to the Seychelles Islands?' That same year he asked 'whether any action can be taken through the U.N. to ensure free elections in Poland, Hungary; and whether the people of Cyprus will be accorded the right of national self-determination.'

At one point MacBride joined Eamon de Valera in defending his old department: 'I should like to echo what Deputy de Valera said ... that the Department of External Affairs was an easy target for uninformed and perverse criticism. That is so. It is so not merely here, but in nearly every other country ... we do not make use of the very valuable information from these organisations ... FAO, OEEC, Council of Europe, EEC.... Personally I have little faith in political international organisations, which are purely inter-governmental. They are tied, such as the UNO ... I think that Britain has done more to help Communism in Europe than Russia itself.... I regard the Convention on Human Rights as being of tremendous importance.'

But MacBride's overriding concerns were still partition and the economy. He contributed vigorously to debates on both subjects, eventually helping to bring down the government. On partition he spoke in a debate on the 'unlawful use of force in Northern Ireland', which marked him off, as he recognised, from the major parties in the Dáil. Speaking on 30 November 1955 MacBride said:

> The events that have given rise to the statesmanlike and constructive statement made by the Taoiseach, are inseparable from the results of the situation which has been

imposed upon the country. The Partition of Ireland, as the Taoiseach has rightly pointed out, is a clear infringement of the sovereign rights of the Irish people.... I do not want to say anything here tonight that may be construed as an encouragement to acts of violence.... I can well understand the attitude of any young Irishman, who considers that his attitude should be one of open revolt against the infringement of the sovereign rights of the Irish people.... I can well understand the attitude of any young Irishman who considers that his attitude should be one of open revolt against the infringement of our sovereignty, I can understand and sympathise even, with the attitude of an Irishman in the Six Counties who is prepared to use any means at his disposal to undo the wrong, but I have little sympathy with those who would, from a distance, encourage in this situation young men actuated by patriotic motives, to endanger their lives and their liberty.... I join with the Taoiseach in appealing to those in our midst who are in an attitude of open revolt, to refrain from creating a situation, in which they will come into conflict with our own people here ... can only weaken the national effort and retard untimely the reunification of our country. I know that the present government and leader of the opposition would reject these views, to secure representation for the people of the six counties ... we are failing in our duty to provide leadership for the nation.[6]

On the economy MacBride said in 1955: 'We are inclined to discuss unemployment and emigration here on the basis that, if we have not got more than 70,000 people unemployed we are doing well ... we never have a true picture by reason of emigration ... the utilisation of the National Development Fund to reduce interest rates, would come within the terms of the Act ... to make loans available for development purposes.'

Speaking on the Adjournment Debate on 13 December 1956, MacBride after some initial heckling, when Seán MacEntee called him 'Uriah Heep', spoke of 'this kind of childish, irresponsible and ill-informed crossfire, as precluding those who take part in it from appreciating the actual problems and the basis on which we have to deal'. He said that there was a complete lack of realism and objectivity in most economic discussions in the House. They were used for eternal political Party warfare and wrangling, by both sides of the House. He said that the economy suffered from an adverse trade balance and an adverse balance of payments over thirty years. The true rate of unemployment was masked by high level of emigration, which saw 319,000 people leave the country during the years 1946-56. He said that they had failed to build an Ireland in which people could live and work. Over the last five years only 1,400 new jobs were created, while 37,000 were lost in agriculture alone. He then said, 'It is that which makes me so impatient with the irresponsible Party warfare which mars any attempt at a constructive approach to our problems.' At that stage Mr Seán Flanagan said, 'This is a three-hour debate and not a three-week debate.'

MacBride said that the starvation of capital and a sound investment policy were the main reasons for the failure. He also instanced a lack of planning and informed technical advice. He had been asked earlier, by Deputy Blaney, why he supported the present government if he did not agree with its policies. 'The answer is extremely simple. We know that the alternative to Deputy Sweetman as Minister for Finance is Deputy MacEntee and we all know that ... not only would you have a credit squeeze now, but in addition, subsidies would possibly also be removed to reduce the consumers' purchasing power, because that is exactly what he did in 1951-52.' He noted that the government had just set up an investment committee. He acknowledged that many good measures, by both governments, were initiated — the ESB, Irish Shipping, Bord na Mona. He welcomed the recent 'careful and well-considered analysis made by the Trade Union Congress' as a realistic attempt to assess the difficulties and put forward long-term proposals. He disagreed profoundly with the government's current credit squeeze, which was causing a fall in industrial production and investment. He criticised the government's curtailment of public works as unwise and indefensible. He called for expenditure on land projects, drainage schemes, afforestation and the building of schools throughout the country. Otherwise, he believed that there would be up to 100,000 unemployed and he argued that it would make more sense providing employment than paying unemployment money.[7]

Members of Clann na Poblachta pressed their three Dáil deputies to stop supporting the government because of its poor economic performance and its action against the IRA. By then Seán MacBride's influence within the party had declined. The national executive insisted on its prerogative to direct its parliamentary representatives how they should vote in the Dáil.

Tom O'Higgins, a member of the coalition government has recalled how before Christmas he went to see MacBride at his home in Roebuck to ask him to propose a vote of confidence in the government, which he did. O'Higgins found him 'charming and concerned with the problems of the Government. But six weeks later, on 28 January 1957, he put down a motion of no confidence and the Government fell. When he was with you, he was forceful and charming, but when the sun went in he was a different man. He went round in complete circles, and in politics he ended up having the extreme republican views he started with.'[8]

The TDs themselves, particularly MacBride, thought it would be a very foolish move to defeat the government and return de Valera to power. MacBride knew that de Valera would deal much more severely with the IRA, as his record showed. But on 28 January MacBride found himself at the behest of the executive tabling a motion of 'no confidence' in Costello's government because of its poor economic per-formance and high unemployment.

In the North an IRA campaign had been in progress for some years. Sinn Féin was having electoral success in the Westminster elections with IRA prisoners, though they were standing on an abstentionist platform. On 26 May 1955, it had Tom Mitchell and Phil Clarke elected to Westminster. Under British electoral law, they were not allowed to take their seats as convicted felons.[9]

In late 1956 the IRA launched a major offensive in the North and attacked military targets. The British put pressure on Costello's government to contain the IRA south of the border. Two volunteers, Fergal O'Hanlon and Seán South, were killed in action and enormous crowds attended their funerals in Monaghan and Limerick. Many public bodies passed votes on sympathy. Costello appealed for reason on 6 January as he addressed the public on Radio Eireann. This time he eschewed earlier government attitudes of a soft approach to the IRA. He said that there could only be one government, one parliament and one army in the State. Within days leading members of the IRA were rounded up and jailed. Once more it could be claimed that political prisoners were being held. The members of Clann na Poblachta rebelled and acted, as we have seen above. The IRA attacks continued into 1957.

In January 1956 the government had received an aide-mémoire from the British government, pressing strongly for the co-operation of the Gardai. It alleged 'a total unwillingness on the part of the Civil Guard to assist the RUC with information or to co-operate in identifying the raiders [on Roslea, Fermanagh, RUC Barracks]'.[10] The aide-mémoire refers to the fact that, in March 1955, IRA training activities were going on at Scotstown, County Monaghan. This information was given to the Gardai and the Irish government, 'yet it appears that the men were allowed to continue with their illegal activities without interference'.

In February 1956 the Department of External Affairs replied to the British, saying starkly that they could expect little co-operation from the Irish on subversive activity: 'Briefly, the attitude is that the Government could not allow information to be furnished about Irishmen already apprehended, or being actively sought in connection with armed political activities and could not accept any responsibility or commitment in regard to the intentions of unlawful organisations which are, of their nature, secret'.[11]

Writing years later of this aide-mémoire to the British Conor Cruise O'Brien says: 'This document was issued under the Second Inter-Party Government, and it clearly reflects the influence of the late Seán MacBride, on whom that government depended for its continued existence. It represents what was to remain the high water-mark (until 1969-70) of Irish government collusion with the I.R.A. This policy was dropped by the de Valera-Lemass government when it came back to power in 1957.'[12]

20

Defeat at the Polls

The resulting 1957 general election was a personal disaster for Seán MacBride. At his party's final rally in Dublin he said: 'We will use all the strength the people give us to secure the formation of a National Government and the implementation of a comprehensive long-term economic development programme.'[1] During the campaign de Valera denied that Fianna Fáil had ever taken the oath of allegiance to the British monarch. MacBride's first preference votes were well down at 2,877. He was used to grim election counts, but he usually had managed to get elected on late count transfers. *The Irish Times* reported on 7 March 1957 that 'At about 3 a.m. today it was announced that Mr Seán MacBride had been defeated on the eleventh count in Dublin South West by a Fianna Fáil candidate, Mr. Butler. The eleventh count saw a distribution of Mr. Carroll's (IND) surplus votes: Butler (+1,383) 6,008; MacBride (+194) 5,390.[2]

This defeat ended Clann na Poblachta's hopes of a future role in Irish politics. Sinn Féin fought a vigorous campaign, drawing on the heat generated in Northern Ireland. It got a first preference vote nationwide of 65,000, and four candidates were elected on an abstentionist basis. The full result was: Fianna Fáil 78, Fine Gael 40, Labour 12, Sinn Féin 4, Clann na Talmhan 3, Clann na Poblachta 1, Others 9. It was a clear victory for Eamon de Valera. *The Irish Press* interpreted the election in an editorial the next day:

The outstanding features of the General Election, apart from personalities, are the return of Fianna Fail as the strongest party in the Dail since the establishment of the Oireachtas in 1927, and the very substantial vote cast for Sinn Fein, with only nineteen candidates in the contest....

The vote for Sinn Fein could be interpreted merely as an expression of 'no confidence' by a large body of the people in all the parties that constitute the Dail. The extent of the vote was, in round figures, 65,000, but it is clear that a much stronger voice would have been raised for the party had it sought an opinion in more than nineteen constituencies.

It is interesting to note that Sinn Fein, in winning four seats, secured just one short of the number gained in the name of Sinn Fein when a party of that name last sought the votes of the people. That was in 1927, and then, as now, the Sinn Fein Deputies did not take their seats....[3]

Sinn Féin had superseded Clann na Poblachta as the republican party. Unfortunately for political development in Ireland, Sinn Féin did not enter the Dáil. Despite promptings from MacBride, it stood steadfastly as an abstentionist party. Although most Irish people now recognised Dáil Eireann as the country's legitimate parliament, Sinn Féin was not yet ready to do so.

MacBride's predictions to his party proved accurate and de Valera became Taoiseach. The IRA scaled down its armed campaign in the North and the new government released the IRA prisoners from Mountjoy Jail. But the government was being very careful as an *Irish Press* report of 4 April 1957 demonstrates:

Twenty-eight university students and recent graduates were taken into custody by Gardai and Special Branch detectives at Glencree in the Dublin mountains. Among those detained were Mr Tiernan MacBride, son of Mr Seán MacBride, Mr Michael Davern, President of the Students Representative Council, U.C.D., Mr Patrick McCardle and Mr Seamus Sorohan B.L. After being released, the students issued a statement saying that 'It was made clear to the police that our party had been on an all night hike and was going to 8 a.m. Mass in the village. We were not allowed to proceed.'[4]

Tiernan MacBride recalls that this escapade was a ruse to flush out the Special Branch, to demonstrate that de Valera would crack down hard on any supposed subversion.[5]

The summer months were never the best time for guerilla warfare, but the IRA carried out ambushes in the North that summer. De Valera was preparing to move against them and most of the leaders were arrested in Dublin in a sudden swoop. Wider arrests followed and internment camps were opened at the Curragh military barracks.

The Taoiseach issued the following statement: 'An attempt is being made to represent the recent arrests under the Offences against the State Acts, as action aimed by the government at a constitutional movement. The twelve men arrested on July 6th at a meeting in premises in Wicklow St. Dublin — stated to be a meeting of the Ard Comhairle of Sinn Féin — were arrested, because they were believed to belong to an unlawful organisation. The men detained were the so-called "Chief of Staff", "Adjutant General" and members of the "Army Council" of one of the unlawful organisations.'[6]

Despite this setback, the IRA carried on its campaign in the North. Clann na Poblachta issued a statement on the government action:

> The action of the government in taking powers to imprison at will, without charge or trial any person it wishes, is a matter of grave concern to every citizen. There is no war or emergency and we do not accept that such arbitrary powers in the hands of the political executive are either necessary or desirable.... The abrogation of the normal law and of the democratic process is not calculated to restore confidence in our democratic institutions. The reverse is the more likely result ... Sinn Féin ... candidates polled 65,640 votes at the last elections.[7]

The voice of Seán MacBride is clearly to be heard in this statement, and his conviction that the policy of internment was wrong, would soon take him to challenge it in Europe.

MacBride tried unsuccessfully to regain his Dáil seat in by-elections in Dublin South-West in 1958 and 1959. At the general election of 1961 he was again defeated, with the Clann winning only one seat. That, even, was due to a strong personality vote for John Tully in Cavan.

The 1961 election was also a disaster for Sinn Féin: their vote dropped to just 3 per cent of the poll and all their TDs were defeated. Pressure was mounting on the army council to call off the Northern campaign. Finally on 26 February 1962, a special army order instructed volunteers to dump arms. A message to the *Irish people* was published in March 1962:

> The leadership of the Resistance Movement has ordered the termination of the Campaign of Resistance to British Occupation launched on December 12, 1956. Instructions issued to Volunteers of the Active Service Units and of local Units in the occupied area, have now been carried out. All arms and other material have been dumped and all full-time active service Volunteers have been withdrawn.
>
> The decision to end the Resistance Campaign has been taken in view of the general situation. Foremost among the factors motivating this course of action has been the attitude of the general public, whose minds have been deliberately distracted from the supreme issue facing the Irish people — the unity and freedom of Ireland.[8]

The result of the general election of October 1961 was: Fianna Fáil 70, Fine Gael 47, Labour 16, Clann na Talmhan 2, National Progressive Democrats 2, Clann na Poblachta 1, Others 6.

Eamon de Valera had resigned as Taoiseach and leader of Fianna Fáil, to be replaced by Seán Lemass, who had fought in the Four Courts with MacBride in 1922. De Valera became the third President of the State at the age of sixty-seven in June 1961. Lemass brought many new people into government who were not of the Civil War generation. In 1959, John A. Costello relinquished the parliamentary leadership of Fine Gael. Richard Mulcahy gave up the party leadership to James Dillon. Early the next year, Brendan Corish became leader of the Labour Party. That summer at the Clann na Poblachta Ard Fheis, MacBride had suggested that there was a need for a third force in Irish politics to offset the two main parties. He suggested that there might be a possibility of a Republican-Labour rapprochement. The Labour Party administrative council produced a document suggesting a 'unity of progressive forces' which would have a say in the next government. Brendan Corish supported it, as did Seán MacBride. The latter foresaw Corish as leader of the new party, with himself as deputy leader, but the poor showing of Clann na Poblachta and Sinn Féin at the 1961 general election demonstrated that the republican vote was miniscule. This made the Labour Party cool towards a third force, and many of its members suggested that Clann na Poblachta should dissolve and its members join Labour. The talks between the two parties ended inconclusively.[9] Labour increased its seats from 12 to 16 in the 1961 election.

MacBride's defeat in that election marked the effective end of his party political career in Ireland. The party struggled on for a few years but eventually on 10 July 1965, Clann na Poblachta dissolved itself at a special Ard Fheis. By that time, Seán MacBride had gone on to other more promising fields of endeavour on the world stage, where he would not be subjected to the whims of an Irish electorate, which he rightly felt, pressurised its politicians to demean themselves, by acting as conduits for state or other public authority services. This MacBride always resisted, saying that he was not elected to the Dáil to get pensions for his constituents.[10]

21

International Commission of Jurists/ Amnesty International

Seán MacBride had been one of the founder members of the Council of Europe in 1949 and had signed the European Convention on Human Rights in 1950, on behalf of the Irish government. It was only natural that, given his family's history and his career as a lawyer, he would be extremely interested in human rights and particularly the rights of prisoners. Through his work in Ireland, he knew how cruel and vindictive governments could be to prisoners who questioned the authority of the state. During his period as Minister for External Affairs, he was well-known internationally. He was also instrumental in developing the potential of institutions that could transcend national boundaries. The European Convention on Human Rights differed from the earlier United Nations Declarations on Human Rights of 1948. It set up machinery to examine complaints about any violation of human rights and fundamental freedoms on the part of those countries signing the Convention. These bodies are the European Commission of Human Rights, which is competent to receive petitions from governments or individuals. The Commission reports to the Committee of Ministers of the Council of Europe, which decides, by a majority of two-thirds of its members, if there has been a violation of the convention. The other body set up was the European Court of Human Rights, to which cases could also on occasion be referred for adjudication. Ireland was the first state to recognise the jurisdiction of both bodies.

The Convention did not come into force until September 1953, after ten member-states had ratified it. In 1955, the Article giving individuals within member states, which chose to allow this procedure, came into force. Both Ireland and the United Kingdom were among the latter states. Miriam Hederman has written that Ireland was so interested because of 'a tactical feeling that such a Convention could be used to press for changes in the conditions of the Catholic minority in Northern Ireland'.[1] Ironically the first case taken by an individual against a state occurred in 1957, and Seán MacBride was involved against the Irish State.

The Fianna Fáil government had introduced internment in 1957, under the Offences against the State Act. Seán MacBride decided to challenge its validity. He entered a plea in November 1957 on behalf of one of the internees, Gerard Lawless. This plea was accepted as admissible in August 1958 and the case was heard by the European Court of Human Rights in 1959. Though the Court ruled that the Irish government had the right to intern Lawless, the case was a benchmark one. A new and vital principle was enshrined: that the European Court could decide for itself whether conditions did exist in a state to justify internment.

MacBride made his name familiar to the Irish public as a court advocate. This aspect of his career was to be ongoing. He continued to participate in some of the most famous legal cases heard in the Irish courts of justice. The case which he himself regarded as one of the most satisfying of those in which he appeared was *O'Donovan v the Attorney-General* in 1961. This concerned some provisions of the Electoral Act 1949, which were declared repugnant, in that they departed from the ratio of Dáil members to population, as prescribed by the Constitution. That case particularly demonstrated his capacity, acknowledged by fellow practitioners, for marshalling and mastering the most compendious and complex materials, whether in fact or law.

He was also involved in two cases which are now seen as landmarks in the development of the doctrine of personal rights under the constitution, through the interpretation of the Supreme Court. One was the Fluoridation Case, *Ryan v the Attorney-General* in 1965. It lasted for sixty-five days. The other, in 1974, was the *McGee v the Attorney-General* Case. The plaintiff on appeal to the Supreme Court won the right to import a specific contraceptive, prescribed for her by her doctor, because further pregnancy might result in her death or in a crippling paralysis.

In 1956 the British government deported Archbishop Makarios of Cyprus to the Seychelles because of his support for Greek-Cypriot union. A guerilla war began in Cyprus. The Greek government called in Seán MacBride to fight Makarios' case at the European Court. MacBride was able to prove that conditions in Cyprus did not justify such action and Makarios was released. This victory made legal history. In 1960 Makarios became President of an independent Cyprus.

MacBride visited South Africa, where he was warmly welcomed by the government. His father had fought the British on their behalf and been warmly thanked by General Louis Botha and other Boer leaders in 1900.[2] General Smuts, the South African leader, who was mediating between Sinn Féin and the British government wrote to de Valera on 22 July 1921. He ended his letter saying 'Ireland is very close to my heart, and there are very few things dearer to me than to be helpful to your people who stood staunchly by mine in that bitter conflict of the past.'[3] MacBride did not shirk his concern for prisoners. Much to the embarrassment of his hosts, he raised the question of political prisoners in South Africa. In deference to him, some were released. (It emerged later that a half brother of Seán MacBride was then living in Natal named Robert McBride. His son was sentenced to death as an ANC militant in the 1980s and got the European Community to intercede on his behalf. Robert McBride, the younger, had his death sentence commuted to life imprisonment just before President F.W. de Klerk visited Ireland in 1991. In 1992 McBride was released and spoke of his Irish ancestry. He has the status of a folk hero among followers of the African National Congress in South Africa. The Irish branch of the MacBrides have an open mind on the claim of common ancestry.)

On 28 May 1961 *The Observer* newspaper in London and *Le Monde* in Paris published an appeal on behalf of forgotten political prisoners by an English lawyer, Peter Benenson. He highlighted six political prisoners: Constantin Noica in Romania, Rev Ashton Jones in the United States, Agostino Neto in Angola, Archbishop Beran in Czechoslovakia, Toni Ambatielos in Greece, Cardinal Mindszenty in Hungary. He issued 'An appeal for Amnesty 1961', to urge the six governments to release these people or at least give them a fair trial. Some extracts from Benenson's long article bear the hallmark of Seán MacBride's thinking and experience.

> Open your newspaper any day of the week and you will find a report from somewhere in the world of someone being imprisoned, tortured or executed because his opinions or religion are unacceptable to his government.... The important thing is to mobilise public opinion quickly, and widely, before a government is caught up in the vicious spiral caused by its own repression, and is faced with impending civil war. The force of opinion, to be effective, should be broadly based, international, non-sectarian and all-party. We have set up a party in London to collect information about the names, numbers and conditions of what we have decided to call 'Prisoner of Conscience', 'Any person who is physically restrained (by imprisonment or otherwise) from expressing (in any form of words or symbols) any opinion which he honestly holds and which does not advoke or condone personal violence....'
>
> Even many democratic governments are surprisingly sensitive to Press criticism....
>
> The most rapid way of bringing relief to Prisoners of Conscience is publicity, especially publicity among their fellow-citizens. 'Democracy is a damned bad system of government, but nobody has thought of a better'....
>
> The members of the Council of Europe have agreed a Convention of Human Rights, and set up a commission to secure its enforcement. Some countries have accorded to their citizens the right to approach the commission individually. But some, including Britain, have refused to accept the jurisdiction of the commission over individual complaints, and France has refused to ratify the Convention at all....
>
> Inevitably most of the action called for by Appeal for

Amnesty, 1961, can only be taken by governments. But experience shows that in matters such as these, governments are prepared to follow only where public opinion leads. Pressure of opinion a hundred years ago brought the emancipation of the slaves. It is now for man to insist upon the same freedom for his mind as he has won for his body.

MacBride worked with Benenson from the very start to set up Amnesty International. His international reputation rapidly gave Amnesty widespread recognition and status and his legal, diplomatic and negotiating skills helped to fashion it into an effective organisation. He became chairman of Amnesty's international executive in 1961 and held the post for thirteen years. During that time the organisation developed worldwide with 3,000 groups in forty countries. Its international secretariat is still in London and Amnesty's Irish headquarters is called Sean MacBride House.

Amnesty International is an organisation that has certainly stood the test of time. It is now a worldwide human rights movement which is independent of any government, political party, ideology, economic interest or religious creed. It is a voluntary organisation with 700,000 members in 150 countries. It seeks the release of prisoners of conscience and the fair and prompt trial of all political prisoners. It opposes torture or inhuman treatment of all prisoners and seeks the abolition of the death penalty. It has formal relations with the United Nations, UNESCO, the Council of Europe, the Organisation of American States and the Organization of African Unity. When most of the world turns a blind eye to the repression and torture of governments, often against their own people, Amnesty International will investigate, document and publicise, in an effort to rectify the situation. It is so often the only hope for those in prison.

MacBride's international legal reputation led to him being appointed as full-time Secretary General to the Geneva-based International Commission of Jurists in 1963. This meant that he had to move to live in Geneva. Seán MacBride, like many public personages, was not a great family man. His first priority was always his work. He had devoted little time to the upbringing of his children and consequently did not know them that well. He thought that he could treat them as he would his staff and be obeyed instantly. He never realised that a parent has to love, encourage and coax his children towards doing his bidding. He had not been over-generous with the allowance he gave Kid, lest she divert any of his money to her own Bulfin family. They had been growing apart for some time, and when he went to live in Geneva, and later New York, he did not invite her to accompany him. Yet he continued to have a very friendly relationship with her, which she reciprocated, looking forward intensely to his trips home at holiday time. She did not seem to mind being left at home. She was very strong-minded, but slightly eccentric. She was a good cook and was a keen gardener, growing her own herbs at Roebuck. It suited Seán that Louie O'Brien continued, with only a short break, to live on at Roebuck. The only activity Kid undertook outside the home, on a regular basis, was to become a voluntary driver taking children to Cerebral Palsy Ireland's Sandymount School-Clinic.

MacBride was a very charming man to those he liked, and if he liked you, you could do no wrong. He loved the good life and would go out to dinner every second evening, funds permitting. But he was never active socially without a purpose. He had no small talk at all, relying on serious topics at all times. He loved the company of women and was rarely disappointed by those he sought out for his special attention. He found that women were better to work with. He found them more efficient than men, being less independent and more willing to take and follow instructions. He liked to hire Irish women when working abroad.

The Commission of Jurists was interested in the international position of human rights. It fitted in very well with MacBride's work with Amnesty International and it took him to places of conflict all over the world on fact-finding missions. Both organisations had to be very circumspect to maintain their independence and resist being used as a tool by various competing countries or power blocks. No government welcomes international criticism on how it treats its own citizens. Most Western governments, in particular, were loath to accept that they would ever be guilty of human rights abuses. The ICJ was a Western-orientated body in the aftermath of the world war. Partly funded by the CIA and in view of the continuing Cold War, MacBride had to tread a careful path to assert the Commission's independence. When he was condemning the invasion of Tibet and the expulsion of the Dalai Lama by the Chinese in 1963, he was very popular with Western governments. During the Vietnam War, in 1968, MacBride was invited to Washington for briefings by Averell Harriman, Lyndon Johnson's special envoy. MacBride later condemned the war. He was one of the few Westerners who visited North Vietnam in 1969, and saw the utter destruction the Americans were inflicting on that country. He had met Ho Chi Minh in Europe in the 1930s.

The International Commission of Jurists was a non-governmental organisation which had consultative status with UNESCO. The Commission sought to foster an understanding of and respect for the rule of law. The members of the Commission were drawn from countries as diverse as Brazil, Canada, India, Lebanon, Mexico, The Netherlands, Nigeria, Philippines, and the USA. MacBride as Secretary General was at the hub of its activities. The ICJ published a *Bulletin* every few months. Each issue included a section under 'News' which usually gave details of the work schedule of its senior staff. MacBride's itinerary makes interesting reading. During a three-month period in 1965, he hosted a dinner in Geneva for the President of India; at the request of the Federal German government, he visited Bonn, Berlin, Frankfurt, Heidelburg, Karlsruhe and Freiburg for discussions with legal and academic figures; he addressed the International Press Institute in London; he was at the Inter-American Bar Association meeting in Puerto Rico; he attended the Council of Europe in Strasbourg; and he was at the 'Libre Justice' meeting in Paris.

During the same period, he went to Georgetown at the invitation of the Guyanese government. He met all the leading figures, including the opposition. The ICJ was asked to set up a commission of inquiry into the balance between the races in all facets of state control. A four-person team spent three weeks there hearing evidence. Among that team was Justice Seamus Henchy of Ireland.

During a similar period in 1966 MacBride attended consecutive meetings in Finland, Strasbourg, Brasilia, Denmark,

Nice, Uganda, Kenya, Zambia, Tanzania, Ceylon, India, Pakistan, Jordan. Most of these visits entailed discussions with the states' leaders. In the June 1966 *Bulletin* an item from the Northern Ireland branch reads: 'This section has recently published a critical report dealing with the new Criminal Justice Bill introduced by the Stormont Government'.

During another period MacBride's work included:

1. Special Report on Angola
2. Commonwealth and Empire Law Conference in Australia
3. Dag Hammarskjöld Seminar at The Hague
4. A United Nations 'Teach-In' in London
5. Council of Europe at Strasbourg
6. Congress of Catholic Jurists at Salamanca
7. Convention on Human Rights at Vienna
8. International University Forum at Milan

In another issue of *Bulletin* we read reports on 'Aspects of the Rule of Law' in such countries as Cyprus, Indonesia, Malawi, South Africa and Spain.

A country MacBride visited in 1968 which made no secret of the torture of its citizens was Iran. He interviewed the Shah, who was so proud that he had all the latest weaponry and torture techniques available from his allies, the American and British governments. MacBride could readily understand the anti-Western stance of revolutionary Islamic Iran.

MacBride also worked for the International Peace Bureau at Geneva as executive chairman and, in 1974, as President.

One Irish woman who went to Geneva to work for MacBride was Muireann McHugh. Her father, Roger, had edited Maud Gonne's *Servant of the Queen* in 1938, and latterly he had been on the executive of Clann na Poblachta. She was a lawyer and was employed by the Commission as a law officer and an assistant to MacBride. During 1968 and 1969 she found exposure to international law very exciting. MacBride was a hard taskmaster and when there was work in hand, time or holidays meant nothing. She made the trip to Iran with him and on another occasion found herself chairing a meeting in Stockholm on his behalf, about the draft constitution of Amnesty International. In Geneva he did not permit his staff to ski, lest they be injured and unavailable for work. He was almost paranoid on occasions about security within the office, lest it be infiltrated, as happened on one occasion, from a South African source. He kept records of everything he was involved in, even telephone conversations. He rarely forgave anyone who crossed him and never admitted to being wrong. The public stances he took on issues did not necessarily mean he followed them through in his own life. But he did not hurt people though he was a cold personality. He never got emotionally involved in any cases he dealt with. This was a necessary part of his own self-protection, vital for a practising lawyer.

Muireann McHugh recalls that the outcome of the Mother and Child controversy constantly upset MacBride. Though he had acted as part of the government, and correctly, he had no doubt, yet the public perception condemned him. On one occasion Muireann's husband, Colm O'Briain, made some innocuous remark about the matter, which Seán did not like. Very shortly they both were invited to a city restaurant for dinner by MacBride. During the course of the meal, Seán produced his file on the Mother and Child controversy, and proceeded to read his famous memorandum, written after dinner with Noel Browne. This he felt sure would set O'Briain straight on the issue. Muireann remained very friendly with MacBride, both on a personal and a professional basis, for the rest of his life. She feels that his contribution to the European Convention on Human Rights, was the single event he felt most proud of.[4]

When it became known to MacBride that the ICJ was funded in part, albeit indirectly by the American CIA, he protested vigorously and later resigned from that body.

22

Nobel Peace Prize

Namibia, known as South West Africa until 1968, was a German protectorate from 1884. In 1915 it surrendered to South Africa, which administered it under a mandate from the League of Nations. In 1966 the United Nations, the successor of the League of Nations, declared that the mandate had expired. It invited South Africa to leave the territory and allow elections to be held. The major indigenous organisation working and fighting to expel South Africa was called the South West Africa's People's Organisations (SWAPO). South Africa refused to adhere to the demands of the United Nations, so the UN set up a United Nations Council for Namibia to seek to implement its policy.

In 1973 the African States of the United Nations nominated Seán MacBride as the first United Nations Commissioner for Namibia. He was given the title of Assistant Secretary General of the UN. The African nations regarded MacBride as an independent and skilful diplomat, who could possibly resolve a long-standing and difficult situation. It was also clear that much of the vested interests in the status quo lay with the larger western countries. MacBride's task was to publicise the Namibian problem and bring pressure on South Africa to accept the UN demand. As Commissioner, MacBride was 'instrumental in the enactment by the Council, as the Legal Administering Authority for Namibia, of Decree No. 1 for the protection of the Natural Resources of Namibia, in 1974. The Decree seeks to protect the Natural Resources of Namibia and to ensure that they are not exploited to the detriment of Namibia and its people'.[1] In 1976 MacBride was responsible for 'the establishment of the U.N. Institute for Namibia, in Lusaka, as the major training institution for the policy-making and administrative needs of an Independent Namibia'.

In his will Alfred Nobel, the inventor of dynamite, stipulated that prizes be awarded annually in various fields of human endeavour. He authorised Swedish institutions to award all of them, except the one for peace, which was passed to Norway. The Nobel prizes have retained a unique place in the world and there is a general trust in the validity of the various awards. Since 1901 the peace prize has been awarded 68 times. Several nominations have been controversial, usually when politicians win. But the Nobel Committee has retained its integrity over the years and most winners of the Peace prize have been involved in peace-creating and caring activities, either individually or through organisations that have this goal.

In October 1974 it was announced from Oslo that Seán MacBride and Eisaku Sato of Japan, were to share that year's prize. MacBride was named as President of the International Peace Bureau, Geneva and of the Commission of Namibia, United Nations, New York. He was cited for 'many years of efforts to build up and protect human rights all over the world'. The Taoiseach, Liam Cosgrave, sent his 'heartiest congratulations'. *The Irish Times* wrote in an editorial: 'Ireland can take a proper pride in Mr Sean MacBride's latest distinction. It is no bad time for the world to be reminded that there are Irishmen dedicated to peace and order'.[2]

In December 1974, when the prizes were to be awarded in Oslo, demonstrators protested against Sato's nomination. King Olav V and members of the Norwegian Royal Family were also booed by left-wing students and they, as well as Sato and MacBride, had to enter the hall by a back door. Mr Sato was cited for his contribution to understanding between Japan and the other nations of South East Asia and for the fact that Japan had a special anti-war provision in its constitution. He accepted his prize as a 'representative of Japan's Emperor and people'. Sato was a former Japanese Prime Minister (1964-72).

The chairman of the Nobel committee, Mrs Aase Llonaes, said that in awarding this year's peace prize to Mr MacBride, the committee was paying tribute to an advocate and champion of an important work for peace. The committee was convinced that Mr MacBride's friends and supporters all over the world would share with him his pleasure on the day, which was actually Human Rights Day. On previous occasions, the Nobel committee had an opportunity of awarding the prize to others who had made a great contribution to the cause of human rights. She added: 'The name of Sean MacBride takes its place in this circle of Peace Prize laureates who have shown humanity the way through darkness'. She said that at present MacBride was facing a new and demanding task as the United Nations High Commissioner for Namibia. He has personally expressed optimism with regard to the future prospects of this work. The world would follow his future work in the service of the United Nations with anticipation and expectation. Mrs Llonaes spoke of MacBride's contribution to the formulation and acceptance of the European Convention on Human Rights and his connection with Amnesty International and the International Commission of Jurists.

She said that MacBride was a citizen of a country that for many years had been the scene of bitter, grievous conflict. His experience had acted as a spur, urging him on in his many and varied efforts to promote international co-operation.

In his acceptance speech, MacBride said, 'It is a happy coincidence that the organisation of which I am president, the International Peace Bureau, received the Prize in 1910. I am happy that the committee through awarding me the Prize, has indicated its support for the ideals of this organisation.'[3] Following tradition MacBride gave his Nobel lecture the following day. In it he said:

> From a survey of the contemporary scene, it was only too obvious that it was often those in authority who set the bad example. If those vested with authority and power, practice injustice, resort to torture and killings, is it not inevitable that those who are victims will react with similar methods? This does not condone savagery or inhuman behaviour but it does provide part of the explanation for the increasing violence and brutality of our world. The rising generation is often disheartened between the ideas enunciated by

governments, by religious leaders and by the United Nations itself and the reality. The breakdown in public and private morality is in no small measure due to their failure to adjust to the tremendous scientific revolution through which we are passing. Churches, by reason of their very structure are monolithic and do not adapt easily. But in many cases they too, have allowed themselves to become allied or even part of an unjust establishment or system. Often they have remained silent when they should have led the demand for justice; often they have resisted reform when they should have been leading the demand for it.

It is the duty of the religious to give an unequivocal lead in the struggle for justice and peace. Those who believe in divine providence should ensure that their religious structures provide such a lead. It is important that Rulers and Religious and Political Leaders should realise that there can be no peace without justice.

Likewise economic conditions which condemn human beings to starvation, disease or poverty, constitute in themselves aggression against their victims. Structures which deprive human beings of their human rights or of their human dignity prevent justice from being realised. Racial and religious discrimination also consolidate acts of aggression. Very often those who are defending the maintenance of the status quo are in fact defending the continuance of oppression or of an order which is unjust. This is so particularly in the regions of South Africa where the political and economic structures are built upon racial discrimination and colonial exploitations.

Seán MacBride made eight suggestions which he said were practical imperatives for peace. These were: general and complete disarmament, including nuclear weapons; the glorification of peace and not war; the effective protection of human rights and minorities at national and international levels; an automatic and depoliticised mechanism for the settlement of international and non-international disputes that might endanger peace or that were causing injustice; an international order that would ensure a fair distribution of all essential products; an international Court of Justice and legal system with full automatic jurisdiction to rectify injustice or abuse of power and ultimately a world parliament and government. He went on:

> Why not stop completely the production of all nuclear weapons? The distribution of drugs and narcotics is outlawed. Yet, self-righteous and civilised governments claim the right to make and distribute these engines of nuclear mass destruction. The issues of peace or war, or the armament race versus disarmament, were never put to the people. The people are never given the opportunity of either knowing the facts or of deciding the issues. Even parliaments are by-passed on such issues or only partially consulted. The real decisions relating to armament are taken behind closed doors by the joint chiefs of staffs or by the general staffs of the defence forces. It is they who are the 'experts' to whom all questions relating to armament, disarmament, nuclear weapons, war and peace are referred. It is even to them that questions on humanitarian laws are referred. They are the experts to whom governments turn for advice on all these vital questions on which depend the future of humanity.

Seán MacBride said that it was easy to criticise the United Nations, but it had to be borne in mind that it was dependent upon the goodwill of its member states and that its secretariat could only go as far as the individual state would allow it to go. He emphasised the importance of the role of public opinion in regard to the United Nations. He went on:

> The more public opinion was interested in the work of the United Nations the further will governments be prepared to go. Unfortunately, however, much of what transpires at the United Nations does not reach public opinion and has little effect on it. Also, it would be useful if governments and parliaments themselves could participate in and follow more closely the work of the United Nations.
>
> The role of voluntary organisations was becoming more and more essential. They were the only bodies that would have the necessary independence and initiative to promote some faith and idealism in the world and they deserved a

great deal more support and encouragement.

If disarmament could be achieved, [MacBride said], it would be due to the untiring and selfless work of the non-governmental sector. That was what Alfred Nobel had appreciated in his day. It was more urgent than ever now. The big powers were travelling on the dangerous road of armament. The signpost just ahead of us was 'oblivion'. If public opinion used the power it had now, the march on this road could be stopped.'

MacBride called for reform of the United Nations to make it more effective as an instrument for peace and human rights. Fundamental changes involving surrender of partial sovereignty should be envisaged. He said that there should be a provision of conciliation machinery that would automatically initiate discussions and mediation wherever the likelihood of a conflict could be foreseen. A conciliation mechanism that would continue to operate during the existence of any conflict that was taking place should also be established, as well as a United Nations mechanism, which would enable the receipt of complaints and investigation, in cases of allegation of violations of humanitarian laws, during armed conflicts.[4]

Amnesty International received the Nobel Peace Prize in 1977 for its contribution to 'securing the ground for freedom, for justice, and thereby also for peace in the world'. Mairead Corrigan and Betty Williams of the Belfast 'peace people' were the co-recipients.

In 1977 Seán MacBride was awarded the Lenin Peace Prize by the government of the USSR, thus becoming the first recipient of the Nobel and the Lenin Peace Awards. This award was the highest one given by the Soviet Union to a non-national. It was presented in Dublin by the chairman of the International Lenin Committee, Nicolai Blokhim, who described MacBride's life 'as a brilliant example of selfless service to noble ideals of peace and progress'. In 1978 MacBride was awarded the American Medal for Justice. Again the occasion was unique: he was the first person to be so honoured who was not an American citizen. He was then also President of UNESCO International Commission for the Study of Communication Problems.

MacBride was seventy-four years old in 1978, and though partially retired was still as eager and impassioned as ever. Though returning from New York to live at Roebuck House again, he kept up a non-stop schedule worldwide. One of the topics that continually took up much of his attention was disarmament. He believed that, unless something was done about it, the world could annihilate itself.

Awards of all kinds were given to Seán MacBride, acknowledging his outstanding commitment to international affairs. He received honorary degrees in England, the United States, Canada and Ghana, and he became a member of the Tunisian Academy of Sciences in 1983.

Catalina (Kid) MacBride had died suddenly of a heart attack at Roebuck House on 12 November 1976. She was seventy-six. Her husband was abroad at the time and rushed home. She had bequeathed her body to the Royal College of Surgeons and was buried in the republican plot in Glasnevin cemetery alongside her mother-in-law. A memorial mass was celebrated for her in the pro-Cathedral. Although she had been born in Buenos Aires, she had dedicated her life to the Irish national cause. Her brother had been a volunteer in the General Post Office in 1916. After being an early activist herself, including a year's imprisonment in Kilmainham, she devoted herself to her husband's causes in subsequent years. Her devotion to and equable co-existence with the legendary Maud Gonne-MacBride was proof of her strength and dedication. Her family became her life. First she reared her children, participated in funding the family budget and supported her husband in his various careers.

23

The Hunger Strikes

Although Seán MacBride played such a wide international role for so long, he had remained in close touch with affairs in Ireland. He had been careful after leaving party politics in the early 1960s, not to get involved again. In 1966 Tom O'Higgins suggested him as a candidate for the Presidential election, whom Fine Gael and the other Opposition Parties could support against the incumbent Eamon de Valera. Liam Cosgrave rejected this proposal, asking O'Higgins, 'are you mad?'[1]

When he was outside the country, MacBride did not speak publicly of Irish affairs. But he remained passionately interested in Irish society and became involved in various organisations and campaigns. He was President of the Irish UN Association and of Irish Amnesty International. He was an honorary life member of the Irish Red Cross, President of Irish CND and Vice-Chairman of the Irish Council for Civil Liberties. He was also awarded an Honorary Doctor of Laws by his own alma mater, University College, Dublin in 1978.

Wherever a good cause was to be found, MacBride was there. Wherever injustice was being perpetrated by officialdom, he stood up to be counted. He supported Ireland's entry to the European Community because he saw it as a way in which Europe, as an economic unit, could adjust economically to the ending of a colonial Europe, without it becoming an economic exploiter of the Third World. He also saw the value for Ireland in a wider market, but he was very concerned about what he saw as a drift towards lowering the country's stand on neutrality.

The continuing war of the IRA and its consequences concerned him and occupied him right up to the very end. In 1976/77 he and a Northern QC, Desmond Boal, acted on behalf of the IRA and the Ulster Loyalist Central Coordinating Committee to explore the possibility of a negotiated settlement, not involving local politicians or third parties. The Peace People Movement also was making a major effort at that time. But the continuing bombing campaign of the IRA stymied any hope of progress.[2]

One of the most shocking episodes in recent Irish life occurred between 5 May and 3 October 1981. During that brief period ten IRA prisoners died in Long Kesh prison, near Belfast, on hunger strike. The British government refused many attempts at mediation as the affair threatened to 'endanger the political stability not only of Northern Ireland, but of the Republic, where emotions ran high'.[3] Margaret Thatcher, the British Prime Minister, became the most disliked English figure in Ireland since Oliver Cromwell. Among those heavily involved in trying to find a way out of the debacle was Seán MacBride. He spoke at public meetings[4] and sought a negotiated way out, which would allow some dignity to the prisoners, some of whom had spent much of their adult lives in jail. Ironically, the British government based much of its intransigent stand, in spite of worldwide condemnation, on a recent verdict of the European Court of Justice. For IRA prisoners had taken a case to the European Court of Human Rights in 1978, claiming they were being mistreated in prison. The Commission gave its verdict in June 1980. It said that the prisoners' claim that their prison conditions and denial of special category status did not constitute inhuman and degrading treatment. It added a comment which the prisoners found to be a 'gratuitous political judgement'.[5] It said, 'The Commission must observe that the applicants are seeking to achieve a status of political prisoner, to which they are not entitled under international law or the European Convention'.[6] The British government defended its refusal to negotiate on the prisoners' demands on this judgement. It ignored the Commission's further statement which said that the British government 'was under an obligation on humanitarian grounds to show greater flexibility over the protest on the issue'.[7] On 25 April 1981 three commissioners from the European Court came to Long Kesh prison to talk to Bobby Sands, the prisoner longest on hunger strike. He asked the prison authorities to allow the prisoners' Officer Commanding, Bic McFarlane, and Gerry Adams and Danny Morrisson of Sinn Féin, to be present at the meeting.[8] This was refused and Sands did not see the commissioners. The whole country was devastated that no way out could be found, despite the efforts of many people. For many nationalists, particularly in Northern Ireland, it was a point of no return for total support for the IRA.

The hunger strikes revisited all the horror of earlier times on Seán MacBride. He tried to help the situation without becoming a tool of the IRA; of the injustice of partition he had no doubt. He quoted John Austin Baker Chaplain to the Speaker of the House of Commons and later Bishop of Salisbury, who said in a sermon in Westminster Abbey on 1 December 1980:

> The squalid pretence that the problems of Ulster flow from the flaring up of mysterious sectarian differences and not from the misery, anger and frustration produced by the sorry mess of 50 years of British rule, the white-washing of the massacre of Bloody Sunday of January 1972, the arbitrariness and brutality concomitant with internment without trial, the hypocritical shunning of the Strasbourg Report of 1976, which found Britain guilty of the crime of torture and inhuman treatment in Northern Ireland, the method used to extract 'confessions' for the political Diplock trials, the killings of civilians by rubber and plastic bullets and speeding ferret cars: all these and many more are equally if not more responsible for the deaths of the hunger-strikers and all the violence and misery that followed.
>
> So long as these beams in the English remain, so long does the English condemnation of hunger-strikers lack moral credibility, even when it is made by those 'speaking as English Catholics'. We have to pause and reflect on the possibility that Cardinal O Fiaich and the other Northern Ireland bishops may be able to see more clearly and certainly with more compassion the complexities and subtleties of the sorry problem.

MacBride did not agree with the IRA's violence and refused to countenance their policies; but he could not 'remain silent in the face of duplicity and methods used by the British in their dealings with Ireland and with the hunger-striking prisoners. Successive Irish governments, opposed as they are to partition, have been put in the impossible position of having to jail and oppress their own young people in order to protect British rule in the North-East corner of our island. A stage has now been reached where this is no longer acceptable to the Irish people.'[9] MacBride's final quotation was from Paul Johnston in the *New Statesman*: 'In Ireland over the centuries, we have tried every possible formula, direct rule, indirect rule, genocide, apartheid, puppet parliaments, real parliaments, martial law, civil law, colonisation, land reform, partition. Nothing has worked. The only solution we have not tried is absolute and unconditional withdrawal.' MacBride added, 'Why not try it now? It will happen in any event!'[10]

In 1983 MacBride was willing to let his name go forward as an agreed candidate for the Presidency of Ireland. But the political parties did not favour the idea.[11]

MacBride saw no dichotomy between having been a revolutionary activist and later a barrister in the state he had originally refused to recognise:

> It was a rational decision. Yes, if you like, I changed my mind. Once de Valera had removed the *Oath* it was possible to pursue Ireland's separation by constitutional means. We probably had the wrong civil war. It was unfortunately about the *Oath*. It should have been about *Partition*. Within 20 years perhaps 10, Britain will have left the *Six* counties, certainly will withdraw its army. There will be unity in whatever form. Three reasons: The paramilitaries of both sides are exhausted. People in Britain generally don't know or care very much about it. British Governments are becoming increasingly unwilling to meet the costs. All of this will produce a political situation.[12]

24

The New Ireland Forum

The damage done to the constitutional nationalist position in all of Ireland, by the Hunger Strikes, caused the political parties to come together in a fundamental review of their position on the national question. This year-long exercise, beginning on 30 May 1983, was called the New Ireland Forum. In it the political parties considered the current state of Ireland, with a view to adopting a set of proposals, 'to which the British government would be obliged to respond'.[1] The Forum consisted of 27 members and 14 alternate members, representing Fianna Fáil, Fine Gael, Labour and the Social and Democratic Labour Party (SDLP) from the North. Sinn Féin was excluded as it espoused the violence of the IRA. It also threatened to become as authentic a voice of the Northern nationalist people as the SDLP, and this was anathema to the participating parties. Northern Unionists refused to be represented, though some came as individuals. The Forum commissioned studies, sought submissions and 'invited oral presentations from thirty-one individuals and groups in order to allow for further elaboration and discussion of their submissions'.[2]

On 4 October 1983, Seán MacBride was welcomed to the Forum Public Session by its Chairman, Dr Colm Ó hEocha. MacBride was questioned on his written submission on decentralised government by Brian Lenihan of Fianna Fáil, David Molony of Fine Gael, Frank Prendergast of Labour and Hugh Logue of the SDLP.

In reply to Brian Lenihan, MacBride said, 'It is essential to recognise that only the Irish people have the right to exercise sovereignty over the country as a whole'. He said, 'There never has been any legal justification for cutting off those six north-eastern counties from the rest of Ireland. There is no historical or geographical basis for the partition that was established in 1920.' He added that 'we have had virtually a state of civil war for almost sixty years now.... The remedy is to remove the cause of the violence.'

MacBride said that Ireland needed a much more decentralised form of government. In his submission MacBride had referred to the Swiss model. He was questioned on this by Deputy Moloney. He answered:

> I think that a confederation of thirty two counties would give a tremendous local option to each county and this is something that is desirable and feasible. It is how Switzerland is being run and it is perhaps the best run country in the world, certainly in Europe, and it is probably also the wealthiest country in Europe. I have lived in Switzerland and I know that every third or fourth Sunday there is a referendum on one issue or another. Why do we not have a look at that? In Switzerland they have had three or four civil wars, they have had many battles, but they have got over them.

He added that the European Convention provided a mechanism for the enforcement of the rights guaranteed North or South. He suggested that the European Commission and the European Court could be vested with a special jurisdiction for Ireland.

Still answering David Molony, MacBride said, 'The tensions in the North are political, not religious, but religion has been used to back them up, sometimes irrationally by both sides ... I think that these political issues would disappear very rapidly if Britain ceased to interfere.' He told Frank Prendergast that he thought the Council of Europe rather than the United Nations, could play a useful role in the North. He said, 'any country can disrupt another country by financing a minority'. He did not accept that the Ulster Unionists had a right to self-determination.

In reply to Hugh Logue, MacBride said that the British had made it financially and politically beneficial to the Unionists to hold out. He believed that the forum should concentrate on getting the British government to state categorically that they intend to withdraw completely from Ireland and to let the Irish people find a solution or to state that they do not propose to continue to occupy or administer a portion of this country after a period of say, five years. He said, 'So long as the Unionist minority feel that they have the backing of the British government politically, militarily and financially, you will not be able to negotiate with them.'

MacBride believed that the British are not anti-Irish, but regard them as an amusing but unreasonable people, whom they must look after. He felt that in the end it would be the British people, telling their leaders that they do not want anything more to do with Ireland, which will persuade the government to withdraw. He added, 'No colonial power ever wants to give up any of its possessions.' Hugh Logue then asked him: 'As a man who has two notable peace prizes, how do you regard violence?' MacBride replied, 'I think violence is justified only in certain circumstances. I do not think it is justified in Northern Ireland, although I think it can be justified in South Africa and in Namibia.'[3]

The final Forum report sought to be most conciliatory towards the Ulster Unionists. It said, 'Society in Ireland as a whole, comprises a wider variety of cultural and political traditions than exist in the South, and the constitution and laws of a new Ireland must accommodate these social and political realities.'[4] The report listed three constitutional frameworks within which a settlement could be considered. These were a Unitary State, a Federal Constitutional State and a Joint Authority. The report was a creditable effort and though deficient in many of its analyses, it was generally well-received in British circles. W.H. Cox wrote in July 1984, 'There is now a consensus among the British parties that the government and parliament of the Irish republic has a legitimate interest in the future governance of Northern Ireland. It is increasingly clear that Britain's future constitutional moves will endeavour to embody that interest in some form.'[5]

At a meeting at Chequers at the end of 1984, between Margaret Thatcher and Garret FitzGerald, respective prime ministers, dismay occurred when the lady rejected out of hand all three options in the Forum report. The manner of her dismissal was most insulting, yet FitzGerald acted in a most dignified way. Suddenly all the years' toil in the Forum seemed a waste of energy. Yet on 15 November 1985, the same two prime ministers signed the Anglo-Irish Agreement at Hillsborough in Northern Ireland. This was hailed as a major breakthrough for the Irish government to have a say in Northern Ireland's affairs. The Agreement was registered at the United Nations and well regarded internationally. It has remained the basis for ongoing efforts to solve the Northern Ireland problem.[6]

Among significant, though disparate voices, which included the Ulster Unionists, Fianna Fáil and Sinn Féin rejecting the Agreement, was Seán MacBride. He felt that it would only prolong the violence in the North. He saw it as giving the major balance of advantage to Britain, ensuring that there would be no British withdrawal.

The Agreement reiterated that only if 'a majority of the people of Northern Ireland, clearly wish for and formally consent to the establishment of a united Ireland' (Article 1C), would such legislation be introduced. The South had a right of consultation on matters within the North, but no actual decision-making authority. Seán MacBride believed that such a situation would not solve the continuing civil war within Ireland.

25

The MacBride Principles

Much traditional Irish-American support for nationalist activity in Ireland has tended to favour the physical force branch of republicanism. Seán MacBride's father, Major John MacBride, spent much of his life acting as a conduit for American money to nationalist projects, as his letters written to John Devoy illustrate.[1] This tendency has presented a major difficulty in recent years during the war in Northern Ireland for the British and Irish governments. Much Irish-American support has been of direct benefit to the IRA. One body in particular, Noraid, has been roundly condemned in this regard. But very many Irish-American groups have close contact with people living within Northern Ireland and have been trying to enlist widespread American support for anti-discrimination measures there. One such group is The Irish National Caucus, which has been very active in many areas of fighting discrimination within Northern Ireland. A difficulty it has encountered is that many people in Ireland and America, who could be described as on the fringe of constitutional politics have been major supporters.[2] This has caused difficulty again for the Irish governments in particular, which are always conscious of the need not to be seen to be in contact with extreme republicans. Charles Haughey, speaking as Taoiseach in July 1980, said that The Caucus had 'many fine people who are not aware of its undesirable associations'.[3] Seán MacBride was one who did not allow such statements to influence him greatly, as he became a major supporter of the Irish National Caucus. He became Chairman of its Irish branch.[4]

In 1983 The Caucus launched a campaign against the

awarding of contracts by the United States Air Force to Short
Brothers of Belfast, because of its reputation of discriminating
against Catholics. This proved to be a successful vehicle for
heightening American consciousness on discrimination in
Northern Ireland. In November 1984, Seán MacBride lent his
name to a set of principles, which it was hoped American
companies operating subsidiaries in Northern Ireland would
abide by. These became known as the MacBride Principles,
and were nine in number and state:

1. The increasing of the representation of individuals from
   under-represented religious groups in the workforce,
   including technical jobs.
2. The development of training programmes that will
   prepare substantial numbers of minority employees for
   such jobs, including the expansion of existing programmes and the creation of new programmes to train,
   upgrade, and improve the skills of all categories of
   minority employees.
3. The establishment of procedures to assess, identify, and
   actively recruit minority employees with potential for
   further advancements.
4. The provision of adequate security for the protection of
   minority employees both at the workplace and while
   travelling to and from work.
5. The banning of provocative sectarian or political emblems
   from the work place.
6. A pledge that all job openings will be publicly advertised,
   and special recruitment efforts will be made to attract
   applicants from under-represented religious groups.
7. A pledge that all layoff, recall, and termination procedures do not, in practice, favour particular religious
   groups.
8. The abolition of job reservations, apprenticeship restrictions, and differential employment criteria, which discriminate on the basis of religious or ethnic origin.
9. The appointment of a senior management staff member
   to oversee the company's affirmative action efforts and
   the setting up of timetables to carry out affirmative
   action principles.[5]

In 1985 the MacBride Principles had been approved by the American trade union federation, the AFL-CIO and by the United States National Council of Churches. A major national campaign was waged by the Irish National Caucus to get individual state legislatures to adopt the MacBride Principles. Various states did have massive state pension funds in American companies, some of which had subsidiaries within Northern Ireland. When the states adopted the Principles, such companies would be obliged to adhere to them. Among the states to so adopt the MacBride Principles have been Connecticut, California, Massachusetts, New Jersey, New York and Rhode Island. The vote in the New York State Assembly in Albany, reflected the standing ovation given to Seán MacBride himself when he was introduced to the State legislature. [6] The voting in favour of the Principles was 138 to 6.

The British government denounced the MacBride Principles, saying that they would stop American investment in Northern Ireland and might lead to dis-investment. The British launched a counter-campaign within the United States, quoting the leader of the nationalist Social and Democratic Labour Party of Northern Ireland, John Hume, as saying, 'The effect of the MacBride Principles campaign, whether people like to admit it or not, is to stop investment coming in, and that is bad for us'. They also highlighted the fact that the only political party in Northern Ireland to support the Principles was Sinn Féin. [7]

The various Irish governments have been sorely embarrassed by the MacBride Principles. During Garret FitzGerald's visit to the United States in May 1985, he 'initially denounced dis-investment as a calculated strategy to wreck Northern Ireland's economy'. FitzGerald later gave qualified approval to the Principles themselves, but emphasised that they should not form a condition for existing or future investment. In 1987, the new Taoiseach, Charles Haughey, 'has adopted a more ambiguous attitude towards the campaign ... takes the view that the Irish government should do nothing to alienate Irish-American organisations, if it can possibly be avoided'. [8]

After representations and discussions in light of the operation of the principles, Seán MacBride reissued the

MacBride Principles in 1986. Each principle was amplified. 'In light of decreasing employment opportunities in Northern Ireland and on a global scale, and in order to guarantee equal access to regional employment, the undersigned propose the following equal opportunity/affirmative action principles:' The amplification consisted of a reaffirmation that full equality of opportunity must be afforded to all segments of the community in Northern Ireland. It spoke of the need for steps to be taken that applicants for work are not deterred because of 'fear for their personal safety at the work place or while travelling to or from work'. It called for the display of provocative sectarian emblems at the workplace to be banned. It called for positive measures to ensure that regulations favouring relations of current or former employees, are not used to discriminate against those from another religious groups. Finally it called 'for each signatory to the MacBride Principles, to be required to report annually to an independent monitoring agency'.

The Principles and amplification were signed by Seán MacBride, Dr John Robb, Inez McCormack and Fr Brian Brady.[9]

In September 1987, the British government announced anti-discrimination laws would be introduced in 1988, which would meet, in general part, practices sought by the MacBride Principles. The government did not decide to include legislation towards positive discrimination. In the two years 1985-87, no new American investment came to Northern Ireland and no dis-investment took place.[10]

26

Speaking of Father

During the 1898 centenary celebrations of the 1798 Rising, Maud Gonne had been invited to County Mayo. In Castlebar and Ballina she received a rousing welcome. At Ballina she was the main platform speaker commemorating the invading French forces of General Humbert. When she travelled north to Ballycastle she found a famine in progress. She set about relieving the distress in her usual determined fashion, confronting the authorities and forcing them to act. Her name lived on in the folklore of Mayo as an outsider who came to help in terrible times.

It was with great joy that Mayo people heard that one of their own had succeeded in capturing her hand in marriage. But the separation of Maud and Major John MacBride hurt deeply in Mayo. It has remained a taboo subject to the present, in deference to their loyal son and the MacBride family.

In later years Seán MacBride often referred to the role his parents had played in the struggle for freedom. He associated closely with County Mayo and, in particular, with Westport, the birthplace of his father. During the fiftieth anniversary of the 1916 Rising, he joined the platform party in the town. Ironically, taking the salute that day on behalf of the government, was a son of MacBride's old adversary from the 1920s, Kevin Boland.

In 1984 MacBride was invited to give the oration at the opening of the Michael Davitt Memorial Museum in Straide, County Mayo. He said, speaking of Davitt:

The fact that he was a Mayoman and that my father came from Mayo probably also contributed to my interest in and admiration for Michael Davitt.... The principles of the French Revolution reached America largely through the United Irishmen and Tone. Later Michael Davitt, John O'Leary, Roger Casement and my own parents were all closely involved in the development of the movement which led to the demolition of colonialism in the world. Indeed in an odd way, because of the close links between the Irish revolutionaries and the Boers and the Indians ... Ireland was blamed for sowing the seeds of anti-imperialism and anti-colonialism in Africa and India.[1]

The fact that his mother and father parted in such bitter circumstances was a lifelong sorrow for Seán. In later years he had begun to speak of his father and mother together. She had written her own memoirs and several biographies of her had appeared. But Major John MacBride was almost lost in the shadows of history. Speaking to an old Clann na Poblachta colleague, Eoghan Hughes of Westport, Seán had begun to express the wish that his father too was deserving of a biography.[2]

In 1987 MacBride returned to Ballina and nearby Kilcummin Strand to unveil a plaque to the 1798 invading French forces, as his mother had done one hundred years earlier. The two plaques now stand separated by a little path.

Despite his earlier difficulties with the Irish bishops, MacBride was a conservative man, who in public at least, held traditional values and was happy to take his religion from Rome.

One of the few occasions MacBride allowed his personal feelings on the hurt endured by his family to break through occurred when Geoffrey Elborn was researching the life of Francis Stuart in the late 1980s. He tried to make contact with MacBride. Elborn wrote: 'Repeated pleas by letter to the late Seán MacBride, for example, with the assurance he could speak as freely as he wished, ended when he telephoned to say that "Francis Stuart treated Iseult disgracefully, and I will have nothing to do with you or your book".'[3]

MacBride opposed the attempts by referenda to liberalise

the 1937 Constitution on abortion and divorce. He was a member of the Council of the Irish School of Ecumenics since 1974. In 1983 he was asked to make a video recording for Veritas, a commission of the Irish Catholic Bishops Conference. In it he talks about his values, the need for the return of moral standards in public and private life, the power of public opinion, and the hopes he had for young people.

I was in the audience at Liberty Hall in Dublin, when Seán MacBride made his last public appearance. It was December 1987, and he was chairing a meeting concerned with establishing the innocence of the 'Guildford Four'. They had been found guilty of bombing explosions at Woolwich and Guildford in England and sentenced to long terms of imprisonment. MacBride entered the hall, shuffling along, a tall thin figure, holding a walking stick. Though quite fragile, he spoke at length about the case before introducing his panel of speakers. Just before that Christmas he was admitted to hospital suffering from an infection. He left hospital on 13 January and returned to Roebuck House where he died on 15 January, ten days before his eighty-fourth birthday. His remains were removed to the pro-Cathedral, where he was accustomed to attend the Sunday Latin mass, sung by the Palestrina choir, on the following day. The President, Dr Hillery said his memory will be cherished with a special warmth by his 'fellow men and women everywhere, whose rights he so ably and so unswervingly defended and to whose welfare he devoted his outstanding energy and talents with such exemplary commitment and generosity'. The Taoiseach, Mr Haughey, said, 'I personally will miss his advice and friendship'. The funeral took place, after mass, on 16 January at Glasnevin cemetery, where he was buried alongside his wife and mother. His family were surprised to learn that in his will, he had left the custody of his voluminous papers and library to his young secretary.

The Secretary General of the United Nations, Javier Perez de Cuellar, sent a message of condolence to Tiernan MacBride:

> The news of your father's death has been received with sadness here at United Nations Headquarters. Seán MacBride was widely recognised in the international

community as a champion of peace, justice and the universal respect of human rights. Indeed, these concerns and the non-violent settlement of disputes, lie at the very heart of the United Nations Charter, of which he was a most eloquent partisan. As United Nations Commissioner for Namibia in the period from 1973 to 1977, he played a major role in mobilizing international support behind the quest for the independence of that Territory.

On behalf of his many former colleagues in the World Organisation, I extend to you, to the MacBride family, my sincere condolence.

An editorial in *The Irish Times* on 16 January 1988 reads in part:

The young gunman came to be the most fervent convert to peace. His commitment to the rule of law and to the protection of human rights was absolute. And his conviction grew that it was only by making the possession of nuclear weapons illegal in international law, that mankind could be saved from destroying itself. His conversion from unconstitutional to constitutional methods in his vision of Ireland's future, was matched by a recognition that the evolution of all civilised society had to be similarly grounded. The lawyer blended with idealist and in turn these were reinforced with qualities of stealthy political pragmatism. The end result — Seán MacBride — in his heyday — was a most formidable force.

A new president of Ireland was elected to office in November 1990. During her short address on the occasion of her inauguration at Dublin Castle the following month, Mrs Mary Robinson, a native of Ballina, County Mayo, said these words, which would have pleased Seán MacBride:

Looking outwards from Ireland, I would like on your behalf to contribute to the international protection and promotion of human rights. One of our greatest national resources has always been, and still is, our ability to serve as a moral and political conscience in world affairs....

The stage is set for a new common European home based on respect for human rights, pluralism, tolerance and openness to new ideas. The European Convention on Human Rights — one of the main achievements of the Council of Europe — is asserting itself as the natural constitution for the new Europe. These developments have created one of the major challenges for the 1990s.

Notes

Introduction
1. *Irish Independent*, 1-2 January 1990.

Chapter One
1. *Life and the Dream*, Mary Colum, Macmillan 1947, pp. 142-143.
2. *Devoy's Postbag, Vol. II 1880-1928*, E. O'Brien and E. Ryan, C.J. Fallon 1953, p. 357.
3. *Major John MacBride 1865-1916*, Anthony Jordan, Westport Historical Society 1991, pp. 93-95.

Chapter Two
1. *W.B. Yeats*, Joseph Hone, Macmillan 1942, p. 303.
2. *We Two Together*, James and Margaret Cousins, Ganesh, Madras, India, 1950, p. 159.
3. *Irish Times*, 16 July 1986.
4. John Quinn Letters, New York Public Library.
5. *Letters of W.B. Yeats*, Allan Wade, Rupert Hart-Davis 1954, p. 630.

Chapter Three
1. John Quinn Letters, New York Public Library.
2. *Francis Stuart, A Life*, Geoffrey Elborn, Raven Arts Press 1990, p. 29.
3. *Irish Political Documents*, Mitchell and O'Snodaigh, Irish Academic Press 1985, pp. 84-85.

Chapter Four
1. State Archives Dublin.
2. Mitchell and O'Snodaigh, *op. cit.*, p. 101.
3. Northern Ireland Parliamentary Debates, 22 June 1921.
4. Geoffrey Elborn, *op. cit.*, p. 52.

Chapter Five
1. *Michael Collins*, Rex Taylor, Hutchinson 1958, p. 171.
2. *On Another Man's Wound*, Ernie O'Malley, Anvil 1978, p. 42 and p. 49.
3. *Dublin Made Me*, C.S. Andrews, Mercier 1979, p. 225 passim.

4. *ibid*, p. 30.
5. *The Singing Flame*, Ernie O'Malley, Anvil 1978, p. 71.
6. State Papers Office, Dublin, S 1322/2.

Chapter Six
1. Dáil Debates Vol. I, 11 September 1922.
2. *ibid*, 8 December 1922.
3. *Irish Independent*, 23 April 1923.
4. *Survivors*, Uinseann MacEoin, Dublin 1980, pp. 326-327. Also *The Irish Sword* Vol. XVI, No. 62, 1984, Michael MacEvilly, pp. 49-56.
5. *Magill*, 'The Extraordinary Life and Times of Seán MacBride', Michael Farrell, Christmas 1982.
6. *Man of No Property*, C.S. Andrews, Mercier 1982, p. 35.

Chapter Seven
1. *Belfast Telegraph*, 4 December 1925.
2. *An Phoblacht*, 4 February 1927.
3. Una O'Higgins-O'Malley.
4. *Irish Independent*, 11 August 1927.

Chapter Eight
1. Mitchell and O'Snodaigh *op. cit.*
2. *ibid*.
3. Dáil Debates, 4 September 1931.
4. *The Vatican, the Bishops and Irish Politics 1919-1939,* Dermot Keogh, Cambridge University Press 1986, p. 134.
5. *Memoirs of a Wild Goose*, Charles Bewley, Lilliput 1989, pp. 108-9.

Chapter Nine
1. *Irish Press*, 11 January 1933.
2. McGarrity Papers, Seán Cronin, Anvil Books 1972.
3. *Frank Ryan*, Seán Cronin, Repsol 1980, p. 64.

Chapter Ten
1. *Irish Nationalism*, Seán Cronin, Academy Press 1981, note 156, p. 281.
2. *Irish Press*, 30 March 1935.
3. *Irish Freedom*, September 1936.
4. *Frank Ryan, op. cit.*, pp. 64-65.
5. *Over the Bar*, Brendan O'hEithir, Poolbeg 1991, p. 212.
6. *The IRA*, J. Bowyer-Bell, Academy Press 1983, p. 150.

Chapter Eleven
1. Irish Constitution.
2. *Ireland 1912-1985*, Joseph Lee, Cambridge University Press 1990, p. 211.

Chapter Twelve
1. *Wolfe Tone Weekly*, 4 February 1939.
2. *Maud Gonne*, Nancy Cardozo, Gollanz 1959, pp. 397-398.
3. Dáil Debates, 2 September 1950.
4. *ibid*, September 1939.
5. State Archives Office Dublin.
6. *ibid*.
7. *Chairman or Chief, Role of Taoiseach in Irish Government*, Brian Farrell, Gill and Macmillan 1971, p. 44.
8. *Irish News*, 14 May 1945.

Chapter Thirteen
1. *Irish Times*, 10 May 1947.
2. Dáil Debates, 5 November 1947.
3. *ibid*, 7 November 1947.
4. Joseph Lee, *op. cit.*, 1990, pp. 105-107.
5. *A Hundred Years of Progress*, T.J. O'Connell, Dublin INTO 1969, p. 230.
6. *Irish Times*, 19 November 1947.
7. *Against The Tide*, Noel Browne, Gill and Macmillan 1986, p. 93.
8. *West Briton*, Brian Inglis, Faber and Faber 1962, p. 62 and p. 114.
9. *The Formulation of Irish Foreign Policy*, Patrick Keatinge, Dublin IPA 1973, p. 95.

Chapter Fourteen
1. *A Diplomatic History of Ireland 1948-49*, Ian McCabe, Irish Academic Press 1991, p. 174.
2. Dáil Debates, Vol. 117, 1949.
3. Dáil Debates, Vol. 126, June-July 1951.
4. *The Irish Department of Finance 1922-58*, Ronan Fanning, Institute of Public Administration, Dublin 1978, pp. 407-408.
5. Dáil Debates, Vol. 126, 1951.
6. Ronan Fanning, *op. cit.*, pp. 434-435.
7. Dail Debates, 1 July 1948.
8. *Séan Lemass and the Making of Modern Ireland 1945-66*, Paul Bew and Henry Patterson, Gill and Macmillan 1982, p. 58.
9. *A History of Irish Forestry*, Eoin Neeson, Lilliput 1991, p. 191.
10. *Ireland in the Twentieth Century*, John A. Murphy, Institute of Public Administration 1985, pp. 123-124.
11. *Magill*, 'The Extraordinary Life and Times of Seán MacBride', Michael Farrell, January 1983.

Chapter Fifteen
1. Dáil Debates, Vol. 97, July 1945.
2. *ibid*, 20-28 July and 6 August 1948.
3. Ian McCabe, *op. cit.*, p. 45.
4. *ibid*, p. 45.

5. *ibid*, pp. 46-47.
6. Letter to author, 16 February 1992. Cf. correspondence between Louie O'Brien (mistakenly referred to as J. O'Brien) and Hector Legge, Editor of *Sunday Independent*, who broke the story in *Irish Times* 11 December 1991, 24 December 1991, 1 January 1992, 20 January 1992.
7. Patrick Keatinge, *op. cit.*, p. 28.
8. *All in a Life,* Garret FitzGerald, Gill and Macmillan 1981, p. 45.
9. Dáil Debates, Vol. 113, 17 November 1948.
10. *ibid*, 2 December 1948.
11. Noel Browne, *op. cit.*, p. 133.
12. Dáil Debates, Vol. 115, May 1949.
13. *ibid*.
14. *ibid*., Vol. 125, 1951.
15. Ireland's Position in Relation to the North Atlantic Treaty, State Archives Office Dublin.
16. *Ireland, A Social and Cultural History, 1922-1985*, Fontana, p. 22.
17. Dáil Debates, Vol. 117, 21 December 1949.

Chapter Sixteen
1. *Memoirs of a Statesman*, Brian Faulkner, Weidenfeld and Nicholson 1978, p. 17.
2. *Washington's Irish Policy 1916-1986*, Seán Cronin, Anvil 1987, p. 241.
3. Dáil Debates, 21 July 1949.
4. Brian Inglis, *op. cit.*, p. 141.
5. *ibid*, p. 143.
6. Dáil Debates, 13 July 1949.
7. *Washington's Irish Policy, op. cit.*, p. 255.

Chapter Seventeen
1. *Ireland Since the Famine*, F.S.L. Lyons, Fontana 1985, p. 576.
2. Radharc, Radio Telefis Eireann, January 1992 (MacBride's last interview).
3. Interview with Louie O'Brien, 19 February 1992.
4. Noel Browne, *op. cit.*, p. 181.
5. *Church and State in Modern Ireland*, Jack Whyte, Gill and Macmillan, pp. 419-448.
6. Dáil Debates, Vol. 125, 4 April 1951-2 May 1951.
7. *ibid*, Vol. 126, 13 June 1951-19 July 1951.
8. *The Leader*, Jack B. Yeats, August 1952.

Chapter Eighteen
1. Dáil Debates, 1951-1954, passim.
2. *The Capuchin Annual*, 1960.

Chapter Nineteen
1. Dáil Debates, June 1954.
2. *Irish Times*, 2 June 1954.
3. Dáil Debates, 2 June 1954.
4. *ibid*, 19 February 1954.
5. *ibid*, Vol. 147, 27 October 1954-16 December 1954.
6. *ibid*, 30 November 1955.
7. *ibid*, 13 December 1956.
8. *Irish Times*, 7 October 1991.
9. *The IRA*, J. Bowyer-Bell, Academic Press 1983, p. 269.
10. State Archives Office Dublin.
11. *ibid*.
12. *Irish Independent*, 1-2 January 1990.

Chapter Twenty
1. *Irish Times*, 5 March 1957.
2. *ibid*, 7 March 1957.
3. *Irish Press*, 8 March 1957.
4. *ibid,* 4 April 1957.
5. Interview with Tiernan MacBride, 14 February 1992.
6. *Irish Independent*, 8 July 1957.
7. *Irish Press*, 6 August 1957.
8. *United Irishman*, March 1962.
9. *Irish Times*, 12 March 1962.
10. Interview with Muireann McHugh, 25 February 1992.

Chapter Twenty-One
1. *The Road to Europe: Irish Attitudes 1948-1961*, IPA, Dublin 1983, p. 38.
2. Anthony Jordan, *op. cit.*, p. 45.
3. De Valera Papers, Dublin 1992.
4. Interview with Muireann McHugh, 25 February 1992.

Chapter Twenty-Two
1. United Nations Press Release, Nam/10113, 15 January 1988.
2. *Irish Times*, 9 October 1974.
3. *op. cit.*, 12 December 1974.
4. *op. cit.*, 13 December 1974.

Chapter Twenty-Three
1. *Irish Times*, 7 October 1991.
2. Bowyer-Bell, *op. cit.*, p. 432.
3. Joseph Lee, *op. cit.*, p. 454.
4. *The Irish Hunger Strikes*, Tom Collins, White Island 1986, p. 374.
5. *ibid*.
6. *The Guardian*, 20 April 1980.
7. *Northern Ireland, The International Perspective*, Adrian Guelke,

Gill and Macmillan 1988, p. 167.
8. Tom Collins, *op. cit.*, p. 130.
9. *A Message to the Irish People*, Seán MacBride, Mercier Press 1985, (based on a lecture given to an American Unity Committee in New York, 22 July 1981).
10. *ibid.*
11. Interview with Muireann McHugh, 19 February 1992.
12. *Irish Times*, 16 January 1988.

Chapter Twenty-Four
1. Joseph Lee, *op. cit.*, p. 675.
2. New Irish Forum Report, Dublin 1984, 1.6.
3. New Irish Forum Report of Public Session, Dublin Castle, 4 October 1983, pp. 1-16.
4. New Irish Forum Report.
5. *Parliamentary Affairs, the Politics of Irish Unification in the Irish Republic*, W.H. Cox 1985, p. 457.
6. Joseph Lee, *op. cit.*, pp. 680-687.

Chapter Twenty-Five
1. Anthony Jordan, *op. cit.*, pp. 52-60.
2. Adrian Guelke, *op. cit.*, p. 143.
3. *Irish Times*, 28 July 1980.
4. Adrian Guelke, *op. cit.*, p. 149.
5. Text from Department of Foreign Affairs.
6. Interview with Paul O'Dwyer, 14 September 1991.
7. *What's Wrong with the MacBride Campaign?*, Northern Ireland Information Services, August 1988.
8. Adrian Guelke, *op. cit.*, p. 150.
9. Text from Fair Employment Commission Belfast March 1992.
10. Adrian Guelke, *op. cit.*, p. 151.

Chapter Twenty-Six
1. Seán MacBride, *op. cit.*.
2. Interview with family of late Eoghan Hughes.
3. Geoffrey Elborn, *op. cit.*, p. 7.

Index